Creative Herb Gardening

GERALDENE HOLT

Creative Herb Gardening

SPECIAL PHOTOGRAPHY BY DEBBIE PATTERSON

CONRAN OCTOPUS

First published in 1993 by
Conran Octopus Limited
37 Shelton Street
London WC2H 9HN

Reprinted in 1996

The right of Geraldene Holt to be identified as author of
this work has been asserted by her in accordance with the
Copyright, Designs and Patents Acts 1988.

Text copyright © Geraldene Holt 1991
Design and Layout © Conran Octopus 1991

This volume was originally published as one section of
Geraldene Holt's Complete Book of Herbs, published in 1991
by Conran Octopus Limited

PROJECT EDITOR **JOANNA COPESTICK**
EDITORS **MICHELLE CLARK, BARBARA MELLOR**
EDITORIAL ASSISTANT **ROD MACKENZIE**
ART EDITOR **KAREN BOWEN**
PICTURE RESEARCH **JESSICA WALTON**
PRODUCTION **JULIA GOLDING**
SPECIAL PHOTOGRAPHY **DEBBIE PATTERSON**

A CIP catalogue record for this book is available from the
British Library

ISBN 1 85029 499 2

Printed and bound in Singapore
Typeset by Servis Filmsetting Limited
Colour separation by Chroma Graphics (Overseas) Pty
Limited

CONTENTS

INTRODUCTION

Gardeners, like plants, invariably grow from small beginnings. Carrot tops afloat in a saucer of water, a plate of mustard and cress seed sprouting on pink blotting paper, or a handful of mint leaves carefully plucked, one by one, from one's own patch of garden – from such ventures, lifelong gardeners are born.

On Sundays, when I was young, I was allowed to chop mint leaves in a suitably child-sized metal mill with a smooth wooden handle that you turned like a musical box. Next, I spooned the brownish-green mint mixture into a little dish and stirred in honey or sugar, some hot water and a few drops of vinegar. Then the best part; tasting it to check the flavour. Finally I would carry it very slowly to the table for serving with roast lamb.

And so for me, growing herbs and cooking with them became as one. I remain a gardening cook and still value herbs principally for their culinary virtues. Yet, as the years pass, one begins to appreciate these fascinating plants for their other equally timeless qualities.

We all know the evocative nature of scent and smell, how instantly we are transported to a time, a place or a person, at the merest hint of a remembered fragrance. Perfumed plants do this superbly and it contributes greatly to their charm.

It may be that for this reason alone, the first herb gardens were created.

Happily, for those of us enamoured of these fascinating plants, a herb garden is one of the simplest and easiest kinds of garden to create. Even a window box or a collection of flowerpots filled with your favourite plants is a herb garden in miniature form.

Establishing a herb garden on a slightly larger scale is one of the most enjoyable garden projects you can undertake. For, knowingly or otherwise, one follows in the footsteps of many distinguished herb gardeners of the past. Pliny the Elder, who tended the box hedges and scented violets in the garden of his Laurentian villa; Sir Thomas More, who introduced a rosemary bush into his garden in Chelsea; and Vita Sackville-West, who planted her rare white-flowered borage in the herb garden at Sissinghurst Castle in Kent.

Some garden historians now believe that many of today's rosemary bushes found in Chelsea gardens are descended from Sir Thomas More's original plant. Indeed, Geoffrey Grigson, the poet and gardener, described plants as 'vehicles of life' and noted how they have been grown in the same place for centuries; as if in response to some memory of our shared garden heritage.

The herb garden at Eyhorne Manor in Kent is laid out in the medieval manner: long rectangular beds filled with a single species of herb. In front is a bed overflowing with varieties of sage.

Perhaps it is their instinct for survival, even in a hostile climate, that so endears these plants to one. For me, their historical significance and ancient value in medicine and food only add to their horticultural attraction.

Herb gardening illustrates perfectly this continuity of ideas in gardening, for the plants that have been grown since before Christian times are mercifully little changed today. Moreover, many contemporary designs for herb gardens draw directly on the past, when herbs were revered as plants with special powers.

There is no doubt that herbs have a power to charm. Of course, they make the most delightful presents, both to give and to receive: a pot of basil, a wreath of bay leaves or a bouquet of freshly-picked herbs please me far more than the most luxurious chocolates. And where is the cook who does not warm to a window box planted with tarragon, chervil and chive plants?

One of the most inspired herb presents that I know was given to a friend of mine by her husband. Early one Christmas morning, working quietly beneath the bedroom window, he constructed a tiny parterre herb garden, marked out with scroll-edge tiles and filled with her favourite herbs. Although difficult to wrap, unveiling it must have been a fabulous surprise.

Yet, the pleasure of planning and constructing your own herb garden is hardly less keen. When I think back over herb gardens that I've planted, I fondly remember my chequerboard herb garden in Hertfordshire where I uncovered a worn silver coin from the time of Edward I. And, in Oxfordshire, where I grew my herbs in a large island border set in the lawn. And now, in Devon, where I decided to move my herbs nearer the house and create a simple rectangular herb garden inspired by my wild herb garden in Provence.

In my own herb garden I am always captivated by the changing appearance of the garden as the seasons unfold. In late February and early March the bright green shoots of spring appear: the fine tendrils of the first chives, the folded, felted leaves of mint and the lacey sprigs of sweet cicely all signal the end of winter. I hasten to protect these welcome omens with a small cloche or even a jam jar, to prevent damage to the herbs from an unforeseen late frost which is a constant threat at this time of year.

One of the pleasures of herb gardens is their versatility: they can be adapted to suit virtually any soil, exposure, size of plot or style of building. Whether small or large, formal or informal, they have a way of settling in and billowing out which very quickly gives them an air of maturity. In a cottage garden (left), plump cushions of lavender form a softly natural complement to spiky iris leaves and the tall spires of hollyhocks. In a more formal design (above), feathery santolina and thyme are used to edge the neat individual beds set among old, worn brick paths.

By April the garden begins to look furnished, with its burgeoning clumps of marjoram and thyme, hyssop and lavender, their bushy new growth jostling for space. Scented purple violets, mauve and yellow heart's-ease pansies and sky-blue violas light up the spaces between the clumps with colour.

In midsummer the herb garden is a riot of growth, resembling a diminutive landscape with its tall trees of fennel and angelica, its hedges of parsley and hyssop and its low fields of chamomile and lemon thyme. Edible flowers bedeck the garden as if it were a medieval mead – roses and dianthus combine with soft blue sage flowers, mauve lavender spikes and the scarlet mop-head monarda or bee balm. Imperceptibly, late summer arrives with the hot, bright sunshine hues created by marigolds and nasturtiums, the yellow-flowering curry plant, and ruby-red blooms of marjoram bursting forth.

The autumn is heralded by softer tones, offset by the grey foliage of rosemary, lavender and cottage pinks whose clove-scented gillyflowers glow among the quiet greens. Gradually the garden slows, the tarragon begins to look tired, there are fewer fresh spikes of chives and I harvest my last handfuls of tender herbs to preserve them for winter use. Some time in November a light powdering of snow or a severe frost marks the resting time for many herbs. Yet some valiant plants such as sage, sweet bay and thyme accompany one through the winter and every cook is glad of them. Even in deep winter a well-planned herb garden is still beautiful, a geometric abstract pattern of grey and white.

I designed my herb garden with simplicity in mind: four beds are divided by gravel paths leading to a central sundial, and another gravel path leads round the outside of the whole garden. Wandering round the garden picking a sprig here and there is one of my greatest pleasures and inspirations when I am thinking about cooking, so it was important to me to be able to reach all the herbs fairly easily. And as any cook who uses herbs a lot will want to be able to dash out to the herb garden at any time, winter or summer, in fair weather or foul, cobbles, bricks or any other quick-draining surface is essential for paths.

Still with practicality as well as aesthetics in mind, I planted each bed from the centre outwards. In the middle went the tallest herbs – angelica, fennel, lovage and bay – to be surrounded by ones of medium height, such as sage, rosemary, borage, dill, tarragon and lavender. Marjoram, basil and other low-growing herbs went in next, beside the paths, and then I edged the beds with herbs that form neat cushions, such as chives and parsley, sorrel and hyssop. Finally I planted the circular area round the sundial with many different forms of low creeping thyme to form an aromatic evergreen carpet.

These, then, were my priorities. Other people's will naturally be different. You may long for a scented retreat full of soft colour and shady bowers, a haven for wildlife where you will be tempted to linger on drowsy summer afternoons. You may seek the restful qualities of a formal garden, large or small, where the cool symmetry of uncluttered lines and restrained compositions of green on green are somehow soothing to both the senses and the intellect. You may feel inspired to re-create a Tudor or Renaissance knot, or to make a garden to complement a particular architectural style, be it classical Georgian or flamboyant high-Victorian, Arts and Crafts Edwardian or thirties Metroland. Or you may simply want to throw caution to the winds and make a garden with pots and containers in glorious defiance of limitations of space or exposure. Or of course you may, like me, be a gardener cook, with the pleasures of the table in mind.

All these different styles of gardens – and infinitely more – are possible with herbs. Yet, despite their variety, herb gardens tend to be highly personal places, invariably planted and designed with special care. They allow for creative experiments with colour, scent and design on a manageable scale, and they yield pleasures and satisfactions for all the senses.

Although my own preference is for the small, intimate style of herb garden, there is no doubt that the large formal garden makes a fine spectacle. What matters is that your own herb garden reflects your own choice of style and plants. The individuality of herb gardens and how they reflect their owners is one of their most outstanding qualities. For me, the herb garden is ultimately a personal garden, created for one's own purposes and delight, close by one's home and truly, the perfect pleasure garden.

HERBS AND THEIR HISTORY

A page from a medieval herbal. Borage was used to allay 'hot complaints' and to make cooling cordials, but it was valued chiefly for the flavour it imparted to wine and cider.

The study of plants has been of absorbing interest to mankind since the earliest times. It is, moreover, one of his oldest and most fascinating fields of intellectual enquiry. During the prehistoric era, when still a nomadic hunter-gatherer, man began to discover which plants were of particular value. In time, as he settled and farmed, it became necessary to organize and codify this learning so that it could be passed on to succeeding generations and hence this essential wisdom was recorded for reference.

We know that over 5,000 years ago the ancient Assyrians, Chaldeans, Chinese and Egyptians each had their own schools of herbalists. Some of the earliest written evidence dates from the time of the ancient Egyptians who inscribed recipes for herbal remedies on clay tablets and on rolls of papyrus. The Ebers papyrus which is thought to date from around 2000 BC, contains over 700 herbal remedies recorded and annotated by the priest who compiled it.

During the fifth century BC, Hippocrates, and later Aristotle and Theophrastus, documented the existing knowledge of herbs. These herbals and that of Dioscorides in the second century AD became the foundation of European herbal scholarship. Dioscorides was a contemporary of Pliny. Although Greek – he was born in Asia Minor – he became an army doctor with the Roman legions. The original of his magnificent herbal, written in Greek, though widely known by its Latin title, *De Materia Medica*, has been lost. However, quite miraculously, an illustrated sixth-century copy, which contains details of over 500 plants, has survived to become an inspiration to every herbalist since.

In Britain the popular herbals of the seventeenth century, written by Gerard and Culpeper, drew heavily upon the classical herbals, but, although correct in many respects, they repeated the same myths and mistakes. Gradually, however, the Greek theory of humours, the medieval Doctrine of Signatures and the astrological symbolism of herbs were discarded. In fact, up until only a century ago, the close link between medicine and herbs in Britain was maintained by the inclusion of the *Materia Medica* in the examination syllabus of medical students.

Plants have been man's principal source of medication since recorded history. Although herbal medicine in the Western world is often seen as a lowly alternative to chemically manufactured drugs, the herbalists of India and the 'barefoot doctors' of China continue the tradition of treating illness with the extracts and tinctures of plants. Increasingly, the rest of the world is regarding the healing power of herbs, or 'green medicine', favourably. And many people, despairing of conventional medicine, are seeking help from homeopaths and herbalists.

Some herbs have, of course, always been used in cooking. The Roman cookery book written by Apicius contains many recipes for dishes flavoured with culinary herbs. And to judge from English cookery books of the sixteenth and seventeenth centuries, herbs were regarded as an important ingredient in cooking. John Evelyn's *Acetaria*, published in 1664 and subtitled, *A Discourse on Sallets*, not only stressed the unique contribution of fresh vegetables and herbs to man's diet but also shared with the reader the author's enthusiasm for growing them. Like every author on herbs before him, John Evelyn regarded a plant's culinary and medical properties as of equal interest. Yet, the practice of treating illness with culinary herbs and special foods, which has effectively died out in the West, continues in China, where health restaurants serve special diets devised to alleviate particular disorders and afflictions.

The magical powers attributed to many herbs in medieval Britain were, unknowingly, partly founded upon what have since been discovered to be sound principles of chemistry. For instance, the practice of carrying garlic to ward off evil spirits and infection does have a scientific basis because the high sulphur content of the herb acts as a bactericide. Herbal pomanders carried to protect the owner from the plague worked in a similar way. And tussie-mussies and nosegays of herbs containing rue and rosemary, carried by dignitaries when visiting their poor subjects, repelled insects.

Every herb has its own history: a herb is defined as 'a plant useful to man either by its leaf, flower, stem or root', and a little research into those uses makes fascinating reading and yields intriguing insights into little-known byways of social history. Sweet violets, for instance, among all their many other uses down the ages, were used by the ancient Greeks as a cure for hangovers. Paracelsus is supposed to have sold an extravagantly expensive elixir based on balm to royal customers, on the promise that it would restore their virility. Woad, used by the ancient Britons to paint themselves sky blue according to Julius Caesar, was also used to dye policemen's uniforms until the advent of chemical dyes. Laurel used to be thought to attract the muse, and poets and writers would keep a bay leaf in their pocket or under their pillow – hence, eventually, the title 'poet laureate'. Rosemary was burned in the streets of London to ward off disease, and in times of plague the price of a sprig would increase by up to thirty times. The list is endless.

The present-day interest in the ecology and future of our planet has encouraged scientific enquiry into the efficacy of herbs. Some of the results are heartening. Feverfew, for example, has been prescribed by herbalists for centuries as a treatment for headaches. Sir John Hill in *The British Herbal*, published in 1772, writes of feverfew, 'In the worst headaches this Herb exceeds whatever else is known'.

Although the Vatican had founded a physic garden for the study of plants in 1277, it was not

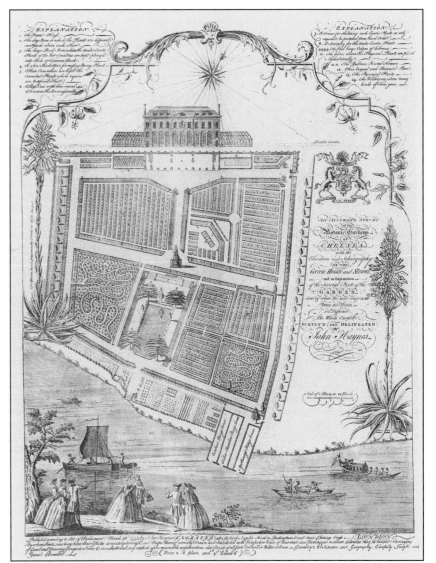

The first physic garden in Britain for the systematic study of medicinal herbs was founded at Oxford in 1621. In 1673 the Chelsea Physic Garden followed, established by the Worshipful Society of Apothecaries for the 'manifestation of the glory, power and wisdom of God, in the works of creation.'

until the seventeenth century that Britain's most famous physic garden was started on the bank of the river Thames in London. During the eighteenth century, Philip Miller, working with the Society of Apothecaries, established a fine, walled garden of specimen beds planted with different plant families to facilitate formal botanical study. Due to the foresight of Miller's patron, Sir Hans Sloane, the Chelsea Physic Garden exists today in hardly altered form and is well worth visiting.

Considerable advances in the botanical and chemical classification of herbs were made during the eighteenth and nineteenth centuries. However, it was not until 1931 that Mrs M Grieve, FRHS, produced her comprehensive *Modern Herbal*, which assembles the horticultural, medical and culinary properties of over 1,000 English and American herbs.

Mrs Grieve influenced many people – mainly women – who began to grow and write about the cultivation and use of herbs. Mrs Hilda Leyel had founded the Society of Herbalists in 1926 and later opened a herb shop named after Nicholas Culpeper, the seventeenth-century herbalist, and contributed, too, to the literature on herbs. The prolific writer Mrs Eleanour Sinclair Rohde helped to popularize herbs and herb gardening in Britain and North America. In 1933 the Herb Society of America was founded.

Many new herb gardens and herb farms were established by the pioneers of the herb movement. Consequently, even though there are some historic gardens in Britain, it has been estimated that the great majority of today's herb gardens are under 50 years old.

During the last 40 years, increased foreign travel has developed our appetite for food from countries where herbs are still considered of culinary value. As a result, cooks have been keen to grow their own supply of fresh herbs. Indeed, it could be said that in their long history there has never been more active interest in the virtues of herbs than there is now. A few years ago, the distinguished gardening writer Rosemary Verey wrote, 'I do not think that there has been a period in garden history when the herb garden has played a more important role both in garden design and in the use of herbs for cooking than it does today'. The enthusiasm of gardeners, cooks and herbalists continues apace.

The Renaissance was the heyday of domestic herb gardens: the mistress of any house of substance would cultivate aromatic plants and fragrant flowers in a secluded formal garden, walled or hedged around with arbors of roses, vines or pleached fruit trees. She would then carefully pick and sort the leaves and flowers, as shown in Lucas van Valkenbosch's meticulously detailed painting Spring *(1595)*, before putting them to innumerable different uses: scenting rooms and stuffing pillows, strewing floors and weaving garlands, making healing potions and flavouring dishes to name but a few.

MEDICINAL AND MONASTIC
HERB GARDENS

Though a life of retreat offers various joys,
None, I think, will compare with the time
*   one employs,*
In the study of herbs, or in striving to gain
Some practical knowledge of nature's domain.
Get a garden!
WALAFRID STRABO, 'HORTULUS' OR
'THE LITTLE GARDEN', 900AD

In Europe, the Christian church adopted a small enclosed garden style known as the 'paradise' from the Middle East, and built them to their own design, either round or semi-circular, adjoining their monastic churches and cathedrals. Although the garden itself has disappeared, the fifteenth-century doorway to the paradise garden at Winchester Cathedral is still standing. Normally, the paradise garden was in the care of the sacrist who grew sacred flowers and plants there for decorating the altar and the church on feast days.

In contrast to the small, private paradise, the 'cloister' garden was a larger, enclosed space, usually built against the nave of the church and surrounded by colonnaded cloisters where monks could study and write. Many magnificent examples remain: the cloister garden of the church of St Trophime in Arles, France, and a similar form at Ely Cathedral, England immediately come to mind. This style of garden was known in medieval England as the 'cloister garth' and it contained aromatic plants and herbs that perfumed the air and offered solace to the monks during their long meditation.

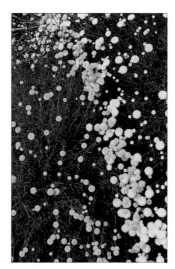

As well as being one of the most popular and useful plants for edging in the herb garden, being both decorative and evergreen, santolina is also pungently aromatic. Traditionally, when winter clothes were put away, sprays of santolina would be laid in chests and wardrobes to guard against moths and insects.

OPPOSITE *This design for a cloister garden by Tim Martin for the Chelsea Flower Show in 1987 includes a mixture of vegetables, flowers and traditional medicinal and culinary herbs, rather like a French potager.*

For over a thousand years after the Roman occupation, medical knowledge resided in the monasteries and religious houses of Britain. These became the principal seats of learning where the texts of classical herbals, usually derived from the work of Dioscorides in the second century, were copied out and amended.

Each religious community aimed to be self-sufficient and, most notably in the case of the Benedictines, the practical art of gardening became highly skilled. A monastery endeavoured to grow all its own food and also a special area was devoted to growing the plants that were valued for their medicinal properties. Usually the medicinal herbs were grown separately, in the physic garden, and they constituted the only form of medicine administered to the sick and infirm.

The earliest known plan of a medicinal herb garden dates from the time of Abbot Walafrid Strabo, in the ninth century, and was discovered at the Benedictine monastery of St Gall in Switzerland. The detailed map of the monastery shows a cloister garth built on the protected south side of the church and the medicinal, or physic, garden sited by the physician's house and the infirmary.

The square garden, or 'herbularius', was divided into 16 parallel beds with a different herb 'both beautiful and health-giving' grown in each. These included cumin, fennel, fenugreek, lovage, mint, pennyroyal, rose, rosemary, rue, sage, savory and tansy.

It is thought that each herb was grown in a separate bed to make harvesting and identifi-

cation easier. The raised beds were edged with pegged wooden boards to keep the soil in place. Whether the St Gall garden was ever constructed is unknown, though its pattern is echoed in the garden design that followed for several centuries. Indeed, the design of the twelfth-century herb garden at Canterbury Cathedral is remarkably similar to the St Gall plan. And, although no longer a herb garden, the little cloister garden at Westminster Abbey formed part of the infirmary garden in medieval times.

The earliest English herbal that has survived dates from the second half of the ninth century. It was written in Anglo-Saxon under the direction of a monk called Bald who lived at the time of King Alfred. The manuscript gives prescriptions for a wide range of herbal remedies and medicines. 'The Saxons had a much wider knowledge of herbs than the doctors of Salerno, the oldest school of medicine in Europe', claimed Dr J C Payne in a lecture delivered to the Royal College of Physicians in 1903. Bald's herbal describes the monastic herb garden of the time, known as the 'wyrttun', in which, among other herbs, gillyflowers, peonies, marigolds, violets and periwinkles were cultivated.

Medicinal herb gardens continued in use up until the latter half of the nineteenth century. As late as 1862 the famous gardener, William Robinson, complained that medical students who were required to collect examples of the plants in the *Materia Medica*, gathered the flowers and buds from his rare plants, making propagation difficult.

At about the same time in North America, the Shaker communities, who had used herbal medicine since they had founded their settlements, established a series of flourishing medicinal herb gardens from which they operated a very successful seed business, even exporting to Britain.

Although most of the historic medicinal herb gardens have now disappeared, the restored herb garden at Acorn Bank in Cumbria (owned by the National Trust) displays much of its former glory and includes many of the plants listed by Thomas Tusser in 1580 as 'necessaire herbes to growe in the garden for physick'.

As far as I've been able to discover, most of the monasteries in Britain today have allowed their herb gardens to decay, though there are a number of very fine modern gardens based on medieval

physic gardens. Westminster Abbey has a little garden of medicinal herbs growing on what was probably the site of the original infirmary garden. At Michelham Priory another modern physic garden contains a large and carefully researched range of medicinal plants that would have been known in the sixteenth century. And Brother Robert at Caldy Abbey near Tenby tells me that he is planning a new herb garden for the abbey. He is a keen cook and so the garden will include culinary as well as medicinal herbs, and will, indeed, embody the advice given in Ecclesiasticus, 'The Lord hath created medicines out of the earth; and he that is wise will not abhor them'.

Many of the herbs that most of us now grow for cooking, or simply for the enjoyment of their fragrant leaves and flowers, have for centuries also been prized for their healing qualities. The physic garden would also contain many plants which are now mainstays of the flower garden, such as roses, foxgloves, pinks and irises. Here they are grown in raised beds edged with wooden boards, in medieval monastic style.

A carpet of creeping thyme, releasing its heady Mediterranean scent as you pass, is one of the pleasures of the herb garden. An infusion of the leaves of both thyme and sage (here the purple-leaved variety) is a traditional remedy for colds and sore throats, while a tisane of lovage leaves (behind) used to be drunk for a wide range of illnesses. Today its spiciness makes it a useful addition to salt-free diets.

CULINARY HERB GARDENS

Gardening cooks have, I imagine, always preferred to gather their own fresh culinary herbs rather than depend upon the vagaries of the market. Even in Hellenic Egypt, where vegetables were usually grown in the fields and sold in markets and shops, herbs such as coriander, mint and parsley were more often cultivated closer to hand in the garden.

During the first century BC, Columella sang the praises of home-grown produce and gave detailed advice on how to grow vegetables and herbs. He listed garlic, mint, mustard and parsley as essential herbs for cooking.

Hardly 100 years later, Pliny the Elder made a similar plea: 'That quarter of the garden serveth our house with poignant herbs instead of sauce, to give a commendable taste and seasoning to our meat, showeth plainly that the master and mistress thereof were not wont to run in the Merchants' books for Spicerie, but changed the Grocer or Apothecaries' shop, for the garden'.

The history of culinary herbs naturally follows the development of cooking fairly closely. Furthermore, until 200 years ago culinary herbs were also considered in terms of their medicinal properties, which may, at times, have led to their overuse. A character in the play, Pseudolus, by Plautus, comments:

'I don't season a dinner the way other cooks do, who serve up whole pickled meadows in their patinae – men who . . . thrust herbs at you, then proceed to season these herbs with other herbs.'

Mint has enjoyed a place of honour in herb gardens and cooking pots since ancient Egyptian times at least. Hardy, attractive and tolerant to the point of invasiveness, it occurs in a dozen or so varieties, with nuances in flavour ranging from apple, ginger and lemon to refreshing spearmint and peppermint.

OPPOSITE *There are so many culinary herbs to choose from, with such a variety of heights and shapes and different colours and textures of leaves and flowers, that it is not difficult to make a garden that is useful as well as pretty throughout the year.*

Early English writers usually refer to 'greenstuff' and pot herbs, meaning both vegetables and culinary herbs. They talk of 'herbes grown in a herber', a small plot or garden containing a mixture of herbs and vegetables and sometimes fruit and flowers, grown together almost in the style of a traditional English cottage garden or a French *potager*.

In the latter half of the fourteenth century, the number of small gardens in England increased considerably. The great plague had left many landowners short of labour to steward their grounds and so they leased it to tenants to use as cottage gardens.

More specialized than the cottage garden was the cultivated plot of ground in every monastery known as the 'hortus'. Here both pot herbs and vegetables were grown together in a rectangular garden enclosed by walls or wattle fencing and divided into 20 or more long, narrow beds, separated by gravel or grassed paths.

Depending on the nature of the soil, the beds or 'floores' were raised or left level. Sometimes the raised beds were surrounded by wooden boards and even painted rails. Even by today's standards the variety of culinary herbs grown in a hortus was impressive. The ninth-century garden at the monastery of St Gall contained a selection of herbs that would delight any cook: black cumin, chervil, coriander, chives, dill, garlic and parsley.

Of course, the wealthy also gardened at home on a grand scale, often inspired by redoubtable female enthusiasts. In the early years of the

seventeenth century, Lucy Russell, Countess of Bedford and a keen gardener, encouraged Giacomo Castelvetro to write his treatise on Italian vegetables, herbs and fruit, intended to encourage the English to enliven their diet. Interestingly, although his book is a gem of culinary literature, all the herbs he discusses also appear in the 1580 edition of Thomas Tusser's *Five Hundred Points of Good Husbandry*, though their use sometimes varies. Tusser, for instance, recommends growing basil as a strewing herb whereas Castelvetro includes it as one of the 13 herbs that constitute his Excellent Mixed Salad.

Similarly, Lady Elinor Fettiplace showed a deep interest in the growing and cooking of greenstuff in her kitchen garden. In Hilary Spurling's absorbing book about Elizabethan country-house cooking she writes, 'Elinor Fettiplace devoted a whole page of her book, *To Set or Sow All Manner of Herbs*, to the question of successive plantings, pricking out, earthing-up, feeding, pruning, cutting and harvesting, so as to be able to pick something fresh all the year round'.

An Elizabethan herb garden was indeed a glorious sight, a treasury of plants of value to the kitchen and the stillroom, usually bounded by a hedge of fruiting and flowering bushes. Dr John Hall, a botanist and surgeon, described his enclosed garden in 1563:

> *'It hedged was with honeysuckles,*
> *Or periclimenum;*
> *Well mixed with small cornus trees,*
> *Sweet briar and ligustrum.*
>
> *The white thorn, and the blackthorn both,*
> *With box and maple fine:*
> *In which branched the briony,*
> *The ivy and wild vine.'*

In some gardens the fruit trees and rose bushes were prettily trained against trellises, and it was fashionable to have a vine-covered arbour on one side of the garden to provide a shaded area for sitting and resting.

Thomas Tusser tells us of the wide variety of herbs – culinary, medicinal and strewing – that were cultivated in an Elizabethan garden. Although we still grow most of the herbs, we appear to have forgotten that some of them are edible. The twenty-one 'herbs and roots for sallets

FAR LEFT *As well as the more familiar culinary herbs, the herb garden at Gunby Hall in Lincolnshire contains an evocative catalogue of names which recall traditional British recipes and remedies of former centuries: including tansy, lovage, camphor and balm.*

LEFT *With its sweetly scented purple-blue flowers and aromatic deep-green foliage, hyssop (flanked here by mint and an airy stand of fennel) makes a delightfully informal edging to a path. Gascon cooks use the spicy leaves to flavour rich meat dishes and tomato preserves, while in Britain they are traditionally added to the syrup of cooked peaches.*

and sauce' contain one or two surprises, including the 'blessed thistle' and sea holly. Violets are also included, and are only one of the many flowers that used to be eaten much more freely than they are today. In Elizabethan cooking, flowers were strewn over sweet and savoury dishes and they were candied and conserved. In Sir Hugh Plat's *Delightes for Ladies*, published in 1602, the many flower recipes include preparations for primroses, cowslips, gillyflowers, marigolds and nasturtiums. Above all, the rose and the violet figure most prominently in cookery and household books of the time.

Herb flowers such as rosemary, lavender, hyssop, thyme and marjoram were added to salads and were steeped in a sugar syrup to make sweetmeats. Fennel seeds were made into candied comfits and every sweetly scented herb was distilled with water to make a perfumed potion or spirit. The Elizabethan fondness for scented food seemed to know no bounds and gardeners and cooks were adventurous in their search for unusual herbs and flowers. It would seem that during the reign of Elizabeth I there was a spirit of delicious enquiry in both the herb garden and the kitchen which would be well worth recapturing today.

The most celebrated gardening cook of the seventeenth century was John Evelyn whose work of 1664, *Acetaria: A Discourse on Sallets*, lists 73 different culinary herbs with their medicinal virtues. In his splendid kitchen garden at Sayes Court in Deptford, London, where he even designed an early glasshouse, Evelyn advised growing chervil as an edging herb because it 'is handsome and proper', and took pains to grow vegetables and herbs that would enable him to serve a salad every day of the year. He produced a special calendar listing the plants to incorporate into salads. These included many herbs with interesting varieties such as Greenland sorrel and Indian nasturtium. He approached the making of salads as an art, emphasizing the importance both of suiting the salad to the person who was going to eat it and of finely tuning the ingredients: 'In the Composure of a Salid, every plant came in to bear its part, without being over-power'd by some Herb of a stronger taste, so as to endanger the native Sapor and Vertue of the vert; but fall into their places, like the Notes of Music in which there

Here horseradish grows next to a clump of lemon balm, whose lemon-scented leaves can be used to add a delicate lemon flavour to a host of dishes, including soups and salads, custards and ice creams, teas and sponge cakes, stuffings and vinegars. Bees love it too.

shall be nothing harsh or grating.'

Evelyn's gardening contemporary in France was Olivier de Serres, described as the Father of French Agriculture, and famous for some important horticultural innovations. His unusual herb garden design was built on a mound or small hillock with a long, spiralling path to the summit, lined each side with herbs.

Olivier de Serres lived in the moderate climate of the Ardèche region of France. Yet, even the comparatively discouraging climate of Scotland spurred on one avid seventeenth-century garden-er. In his book, *The Scots Gard'ner*, published in 1683, John Reid advised:

'Of sweet herbes: as, Clary by seeds and offsets in Aprile; at which time you may slip and set Tansie, Sage, Cost, Mint, Balme, Winter Savory, Thyme, Penniroyall, Wild Marjorum, Maudlin, Fennell, etc. Prune their tops and fibres, and plant in garden soil, 8 rowes in the bed; they all continue long: but cutting their tops in growing time makes them more durable: and cut them all within a handful of the ground at August, that they may recover against the winter'.

John Reid dedicates his book 'To all the Ingenious Planters in Scotland' and proceeds to give sound advice on how to cultivate tender herbs such as basil, dill and rosemary, that in ideal circumstances prefer to grow in a much warmer Mediterranean climate.

During the heyday of kitchen gardening, in Victorian England, herbs regained some of their earlier importance. The most familiar and often-used English herbs, mint, parsley and sage, were to be found in almost every garden. In the walled kitchen gardens of grand houses, more unusual culinary herbs, such as tarragon and fennel, were planted in the protected south- and west-facing borders at the foot of the wall; and glass cloches and leaded lights enabled the gardener to extend the season of many culinary herbs in order to satisfy the needs of the country-house kitchen.

From the 1880s onwards a more naturalistic style of garden design was introduced under the influence of William Robinson and Gertrude Jekyll. Herbs began to be reassessed as attractive plants in their own right. The few herb gardens that Gertrude Jekyll designed contained a mixture of culinary and medicinal plants. She had an exciting approach to planting, and created great swathes of foliage by planting a dozen or more plants at a time, thereby increasing their impact and producing a more natural effect.

The great revival of interest in growing herbs that began between World Wars I and II has led to many new herb gardens being established. Shortages of patent medicines based on chemical products during both wars prompted a return to traditional herbal remedies. This trend for natural medicine continues today.

Some of the most handsome culinary herb gardens in the British Isles have been created by talented cooks. In the Northamptonshire village of Farthinghoe, Nicola Cox and her husband, Simon, run a flourishing wine and food school in the former rectory. They have gradually restored the magnificent walled kitchen garden where Nicola has planted a charming culinary herb garden. Large enough to provide plenty of herbs for both her cooking classes and her family's meals, the design is based on a series of diagonal borders separated by gravel paths. The narrow beds, from which it is easy to gather the herbs, are edged with Cotswold stone. The wide variety of culinary plants includes bronze fennel and Egyptian onions, angelica and lemon thyme, heart's-ease pansies and horseradish, and they are planted with a fine regard for contrast of leaf and colour and so form a most attractive area of the garden. A similar, though more extensive, culinary herb garden has recently been created by Dorinna Allen at Ballymaloe House, near Cork, in southern Ireland. Once again, the garden is intended to supply the needs of a cooking school and a family, plus, in this case, the requirements of her parents-in-law's beautiful hotel. Starting with a quarter of an acre of virgin meadow, sheltered by a belt of mature trees on one side and a high hedge on another, Dorinna has created a classic, symmetrical design of twenty geometrically shaped herb

beds surrounded by low, clipped box hedging and separated by gravel paths. A summer house at one end of the garden is balanced by an antique wrought iron seat and a sundial placed at the other. Here, on a summer's day, a cook can sit in quiet contemplation, dreaming of dishes inspired by this sumptuous display of herbal beauty. A bed of crimson-red orache stands next to a tower of flowering fennel, a tapestry of orange and yellow nasturtiums is backed by a froth of French tarragon and a carpet of purple sage. This, indeed, is a cook's dream of a herb garden.

The seedheads of garlic add their spiralling arabesques to the herb garden in autumn. Highly esteemed all over the world and way back into the mists of time, garlic is indispensable in many kitchens and an essential ingredient in Mediterranean cooking. It is also rich in vitamin C, has strong antiseptic qualities and reduces blood cholesterol levels.

FORMAL HERB GARDENS

Plays of light and shade can be used to add depth to a formal axis. Here at Cranborne Manor in Dorset a pale stone sundial is picked out against a dark yew backdrop, while mounds of grey-green santolina complete the tonal range.

OPPOSITE *Rosemary Verey's delightful herb garden at Barnsley House in Gloucestershire is cleverly divided into diamonds and triangles by clipped box borders. The central diamonds contain herbs such as sage, lovage and rosemary. Around the edges grow chives and pennyroyal.*

Most of us find the ordered symmetry of a formal herb garden pleasing. The artful arrangement of straight lines and curves satisfies both the eye and the brain, and even gardeners who prefer a more informal style usually admit an admiration for a well-groomed formal garden. For the formality of clipped hedges and neat paths with tidy planting can produce an atmosphere of peace and tranquillity in a garden – as if man and the unruly forces of nature have come to terms with each other to produce harmony.

From the damask roses and myrtle bushes of the ancient Persian paradise gardens, to the clipped box trees and rosemary hedges that surrounded beds of violets in the garden of Pliny's Laurentian villa, formal gardens have traditionally been the work of herb gardeners who take pride in growing their plants following a plan or pattern. Indeed, herbs such as rosemary, lavender and thyme which grow in clumps are ideally suited to a formal garden arrangement, offering not only a structured form but an opportunity for creating a delightful collection of herbal aromas. Such formal gardens are in sharp contrast to the freely romantic style of the unstructured medieval 'flowery mead' or meadow.

Court life has always favoured the formal garden as a private space where the sovereign and friends could spend time in gentle exercise or leisure. In Italy and France a palace garden invariably contained a pavilion or 'gloriette' large enough for dining or music-making. Good King René of France (1409–1480), a gifted gardener and patron of the arts, was said to have spent much of his later life writing and drawing in his elegant little garden house.

In 1447, in the Royal garden at Greenwich, an elevated and galleried arbour was built for the Queen so that she could admire the hedged garden below. And in the first year of the following century Henry VII fashioned a new garden at Richmond Palace to welcome Catherine of Aragon; it was 'under the King's windows, Queen's, and other estates, most fair and pleasant gardens, with royal knots alleyed and herbed'.

Within a few decades the style of garden known as the 'knot' had become highly popular. The classic knot garden is a level, rectangular bed planted in an intricate pattern, often based on a maze or a sinuous knotted coil of rope, that is delineated by means of a low, clipped hedge. The spaces between the hedges were either planted with herbs or filled with coloured gravels and sand. The whole effect was reminiscent of a faceted jewel or a tapestry cushion. Though fun to admire at ground level, the knot garden was best viewed from a nearby upper window where the overall pattern could be seen more clearly.

At Hampton Court, Henry VIII employed an army of gardeners to lay out elaborately designed gardens, planted with miniature box hedges and aromatic herbs that were clipped to shape. Although no longer miniature, his magnificent maze is still growing today.

The highly decorative designs of a Tudor knot garden resemble the embroidery patterns of the

time. These, in turn, were inspired by the architectural decoration known as strapwork.

In fashionable gardens of the seventeenth century, the Italian-inspired knot garden gave way to the 'parterre' style from France. The parterre garden was usually a symmetrical arrangement of knot gardens separated by paths of fine gravel or raked sand. In the *parterre de broiderie* garden, the herbs planted within the low, clipped hedges were trimmed to an even height so that the effect was like that of a subtle, embossed embroidery.

By the time of the reign of William and Mary (1689–1702), an alternative form of parterre developed which is known as *Parterre Anglais*. Here the herbs and aromatic plants enclosed by the low, clipped hedges are allowed to grow and flower in a more relaxed style. Large houses had parterre gardens built on the south- or west-facing sides so that the ladies of the house could step straight into the decorative enclosed garden.

The next resurgence of interest in the formal herb garden began around the beginning of the present century. Gertrude Jekyll, renowned for her strong, simple garden design and planting schemes of subtle foliage and colour, designed a few herb gardens, all of them in a formal style. One of these designs, for Knebworth House in Hertfordshire, was the subject of an extraordinary and historic discovery in the early 1980s. The gardens at Knebworth were then undergoing restoration, and in the course of his work a young gardener found a plan dated 1907 for a herb garden. He was astonished to discover that it was the work of Gertrude Jekyll. Edwin Lutyens, the celebrated architect and her great associate, had married a daughter of the family (much to their disapproval) in 1897, but no one had ever suspected that Miss Jekyll had drawn up any plans for Knebworth, nor did any evidence exist to suggest that this design had ever been carried out. So it was that, over seventy years after it had been conceived, Miss Jekyll's scheme for the herb garden at Knebworth was finally brought to fruition. Her design, which was carried out to the letter, is based on five interlocking circles edged with concentric rings of brick. Lavender in the centre bed and rosemary in the satellite beds provide a strong architectural framework to the planting, with clipped rosemary linking the circles and a variety of other herbs, mostly perennials,

filling the gaps. This herb garden is a very fine and beautiful example of a formal layout that is carefully ordered and yet at the same time unconventional in design.

The considerable interest in herb gardening of the last 50 years has resulted in a revival of older styles of formal herb garden. Today in Britain there are many examples of both knot and parterre gardens to be found. Two particularly fine parterre gardens, each with immaculate box hedges, are to be seen at Hatfield House in Hertfordshire and at the Tradescant Garden at the Museum of Garden History in Lambeth, London.

In Kent, the lovely garden at Sissinghurst Castle, planted with culinary and medicinal herbs by Vita Sackville-West, has inspired countless herb gardeners. The last of the gardens at Sissinghurst to be planted, it was begun in 1938, then replanted and enlarged after the war, when it expanded from a dozen or so herbs for the kitchen to twenty beds arranged in a traditional cross-shaped design. The formal herb garden also works well in a public situation as illustrated by the delightful garden designed by John Codrington for Emmanuel College, Cambridge: a commission for which he was recommended, as it happens, by Vita Sackville-West. Based on an early seventeenth-century design, this large formal garden was also inspired by John Codrington's realistic appreciation of the average student's tendency to cut corners: 'Having been an undergraduate myself, I knew that no undergraduate, when late for a lecture, could ever go round a corner without cutting it off, so I drew straight lines from every door in the court to every other door.' Three triangular beds edged with box are subdivided into smaller compartments by a network of box hedges. Each of these small plots is filled with a single species of herb or with coloured chippings. The herbs, chosen chiefly for their ornamental foliage, include some rarities such as dwarf white lavender and the native medicinal herb elecampane, a tall, architectural and very good-tempered perennial which used to be made into an infusion for the treatment of consumption.

A monochrome geometrical knot outlined in box is the ultimate in elegant restraint.

SCENTED HERB GARDENS

A scented herb garden is the ultimate pleasure garden, planted and maintained for the delectation of the senses, yet, a garden of 'use and delight' according to William Lawson's *The Country Housewife's Garden* of 1618.

The loveliest scented herb gardens are sheltered spaces, usually enclosed so that the perfumes from the aromatic leaves and fragrant flowers are trapped in the warm, still air. For most people a scented garden is an enchanted place, a blissful sanctuary.

As far as we know, the earliest scented gardens were built in the courtyards of Persian houses over 2,000 years ago. These gardens were generally square or rectangular, and often they were divided into four by streams flowing from a central fountain. The name for these enclosed gardens was *pairidaeza*, the origin of our word 'paradise'. The Persians, who were superb gardeners, required three main qualities of their paradises: running water, shade and scent.

It was through the Byzantine church that such gardens found their way into western Europe, initially in the form of the cloister gardens soon to be found in every monastery. The idea of a walled, perfumed garden found ready echoes in the medieval Christian tradition, accustomed as it was to viewing the whole of creation in symbolic terms. Biblical references, from the Garden of Eden to the *Song of Songs*, had by now confirmed such gardens as images of Paradise itself.

In 1260 Albertus Magnus, a Dominican monk, specified the requirements of a perfect pleasure

What could be more delightful to all the senses, or more evocative of the long and fascinating history of herb gardens, than a walled garden filled with fragrant herbs and flowers? Havens for people and wildlife, they are of course useful as well. Bergamot and marigolds (above) are both valuable ingredients in traditional pot-pourris: marigolds chiefly for their colour, and bergamot flowers and leaves for their heady scent. Bergamot flowers share with hyssop (opposite) the virtue of retaining their perfume when dried. In this enclosed garden the combined fragrances are intoxicating.

garden: there should be a fountain and a lawn of 'every sweet-smelling herb such as rue, and sage and basil, and likewise all sorts of flowers, as the violet, columbine, lily, rose, iris and the like'. He also suggested that 'Behind the lawn there may be great diversity of medicinal and scented herbs, not only to delight the sense of smell by their perfume but to refresh the sight with their flowers'.

The rose had been introduced into western Europe by the crusaders. In fact, the original meaning of the word rosary is a round rose garden dedicated to the Virgin Mary. Although the earliest rosaries were built on holy ground, sixteenth-century paintings show that the style was adopted in private gardens where rose gardens and arbours were built by royalty and the rich.

Circular rose beds were commonly surrounded by plaited hurdles and the roses were trained over pergolas, arches and trellises to make an arbour. The rose became a sacred flower and the symbol of joy and love. Paintings and allegorical tales of the time portray young men transfixed by the beauty and scent of the flower.

The other sacred flower of the early Christian church was the beautiful and highly scented Madonna lily, *Lilium candidum*. In monastery gardens, roses and lilies were grown together with specially aromatic herbs such as lavender and rosemary. Garden historians believe that the medieval romance garden and the Renaissance love garden were primarily rose and herb gardens, as much esteemed for their aesthetic qualities as for their usefulness.

The heyday of the scented garden was undoubtedly during the reign of Elizabeth I when public taste enjoyed sweetly scented food, rooms and clothes. The mistress of an Elizabethan manor house cultivated fragrant flowers and aromatic plants in a secluded formal garden – usually hedged with rosebriars and fruit trees – not only for the pleasure of walking and sitting there, but also to provide the ingredients for her stillroom. Here, she prepared 'sweet waters' from rose petals and rosemary flowers and healing lotions from the stems of the Madonna lily and spikes of lavender. Aromatic herbs like hyssop and rue were grown for strewing over the floors of rooms to purify the air, and their dried flowers were stuffed into cushions and pillows to encourage unbroken sleep.

With the arrival, in the eighteenth century, of the landscape school of gardening, exemplified by Capability Brown and Humphry Repton, the enclosed scented garden disappeared from many English gardens. However, during the nineteenth century, the public appreciation of a more naturalistic approach to the garden and an awareness of the beauty of individual flowers was awakened by John Ruskin. He influenced the work of the Pre-Raphaelites whose paintings often depicted romantic scenes of love-struck people wearing or holding blooms of English flowers like the rose and the lily. The social reformer William Morris used English flowers such as the honeysuckle and the hop as a basis for his designs for fabric and wallpaper, many of which are still popular today. At that time large Victorian gardens became a series of outdoor rooms which included a kitchen garden, a flower garden, a rose garden and so on. In many houses a splendid glass conservatory became a scented garden with climbing roses, gardenias and lilies luxuriating in the heat. It was customary for pots of scented-leaved geraniums to be carried into the house to sweeten the drawing room and to decorate the dining table.

At the same time, one of the century's greatest gardeners, William Robinson, preached in his horticultural journal, *The Garden*, the merits of individual plants. He was strongly opposed to the practice of carpet bedding – much in vogue at the time – where annual flowers are bedded out in regimented rows. Robinson favoured a natural approach to gardening as advocated in his book,

Many herbs with aromatic leaves do not release their fragrance until bruised or crushed. At Denmans in Sussex, paving stones are interspersed at random with drifts of chamomile, creeping thyme and other low-growing herbs.

OPPOSITE *The lily and the rose, often growing together, were the most prized of all flowers in medieval gardens. Charged with symbolism, both spiritual and erotic, they were treasured as much for their fragrance as for their beauty. Every part of the plants had its use, and the petals in particular would be strewn on floors to perfume the air or used to make pot-pourri or beautiful scent.*

The Wild Garden, published in 1870. In his own garden at Gravetye Manor in Sussex he paved the small, enclosed flower garden with old London flagstones and planted the beds with highly perfumed carnations and fragrant climbing roses – two of his favourite flowers. He planted carpets of sweetly scented violets as ground cover in beds of hardy plants. In 1895 Robinson wrote the foreword to *Scented Flowers and Fragrant Leaves* by Donald Macdonald.

When the Arts and Crafts Movement became established during the latter half of the century, its influence on architects and gardeners could be clearly seen. There was an emphasis on English craftsmanship in the widespread use of brick and untreated wood in a style that harked back to Tudor times. The distinguished work of Sir Edwin Lutyens and Gertrude Jekyll influenced several generations of gardeners, and many English gardens still retain the obvious Jekyll charac-teristics of strong, simple design and carefully detailed planting.

In the present century, the revival of herb gardening which was fostered by members of the herb movement has left a legacy of fine scented herb gardens. One of my favourites belongs to a friend in London who owns a tall, narrow house. The glass doors of her second-floor sitting room open onto a balcony and a circular staircase which leads down to the small square herb garden at ground level. Here, a round, brick terrace is surrounded by narrow beds of herbs and fragrant plants. The walls of the garden are clothed in summer jasmine and honeysuckle, and pots of lilies, scented roses and basil plants stand at the foot of the steps. On a late summer's evening, as you climb the staircase through a cloud of heavenly scent that drifts up from the garden, you can gaze down on the star-like flowers of the poet's jasmine and the gleaming satin petals of the Madonna lilies which face skywards, exuding their powerful perfume. This delightful garden truly recaptures the feel of the ancient scented herb garden: sheltered, enclosed and tranquil, the air suffused with scent. Yet it is not only ornamental, for underlying its fragrance and beauty is the practical nature of the herbs, with their medicinal and culinary uses. William Lawson would be pleased that over 350 years later there are still such gardens of 'use and delight'.

CREATING A HERB GARDEN

The Knotte Garden Serveth for Pleasure:
The Potte Garden for Profitte.
HORMAN, 1519

Your dream herb garden may already exist in your mind's eye and it may only be a matter of time, money and effort to make it a reality. For those of you, though, who feel short of inspiration, my advice would be to start by visiting existing herb gardens, consult books on herb gardens and examine herb garden designs of the past. Not only will this help you to clarify your ideas about your future herb garden, but sometimes you will also discover an established design that is both attractive and appropriate for your situation.

Quite often your house itself can lead you towards the right garden design. If you live in an old house, then the period or style of its architecture may inspire you to take your herb garden style from the same time. For example, a red-brick Edwardian house, influenced by the Arts and Crafts Movement, would incline one towards a brick-paved herb garden with a bower or pergola made from dark-stained wood which would complement the house. Occasionally, however, a blend of period styles can work well, such as a simple interpretation of a *Parterre de Broderie* built in the courtyard of an ultra-modern house.

First, though, it's only sensible to consider the practicalities of a design. How much time do you wish to spend on the weeding and maintenance of your herb garden? Sometimes it is more convenient to construct an intricate herb garden in two stages, starting with the central part of a strong design and enlarging it by adding extra borders later, when you have more time. In my own garden, the design has changed slightly over the years because the herb beds spread a little every time I add more plants. Of course, some garden designs allow for slight changes in the dimensions or arrangement of the borders as the garden becomes established, while other designs are handsome because their formal style is fixed and remains unchanged with the passage of time.

Only a year after I had built my herb garden I changed my mind about the paths because I found that the lawn paths with their neatly trimmed edges took longer to maintain than the herb borders themselves. So I sliced off the layer of turf with a spade and laid gravel over matting (landscape fabric) that requires hardly any maintenance to keep it looking attractive.

The position and site of a herb garden play a vital role in how well the plants grow. In the early 1900s, Frances A Bardswell wrote in *The Herb Garden*, 'The one thing most needful for the Herb-garden is sunshine'. Since the majority of herbs prosper in full sun it is clearly desirable to design your garden to face or slope south in order

A simple trellis arch wreathed with roses cannot fail to lend enchantment to the view. It also provides the practical benefit of shade for comfortable summer seating in your herb garden.

to catch the sun for as much of the day as possible. This, however, is a counsel of perfection and many herb gardens – mine included – grow perfectly well with only half a day's sun. Herbs are wonderfully accommodating plants and, depending on the latitude, they often withstand partial shade surprisingly well. Even if all you can offer is a light but sunless backyard, you can still grow herbs. Simply choose moisture-loving herbs such as sorrel, chives and angelica.

When drawing up your plan, use squared paper and work out the best scale – 1m (3ft) to 2.5cm (1in) usually works well. Make sure that you include all nearby walls, buildings and fences as they affect the quality of light and the feel of the garden. Work out where north is and show it on your plan so that you can take account of the direction of the sun when positioning the herbs.

One of the most appealing aspects of a herb garden is its private air of calm, offering a retreat from the cares of the world. This atmosphere of repose is sometimes easier to create in an enclosed garden, so it is wise to consider the boundaries of your herb garden. Should you grow a hedge or erect walls or fences? These will also shelter the plants and help to create a beneficial micro-climate for the more tender herbs. Existing walls and fences could possibly be extended – perhaps at a lower height – to help enclose the garden or, if necessary, their appearance might be improved by adding a pretty wooden trellis or an arched entrance that will frame a visitor's first glimpse of the garden.

How important are the paths in your design? In some gardens they play a minor role, in others they are designed to be as prominent as the beds of herbs. Do you favour paved, gravel or grassed walkways? Or would brick be the best choice? In a meadow-style herb garden, stepping stones of paving slabs or sections of tree trunks can work well. If it is at all possible make sure that your choice of paving blends with the material of any nearby buildings.

Defining the herb beds requires special consideration. Low, neat hedges of dwarf box look charming but need a lot of maintenance. I like chive and parsley edgings because they more or less look after themselves and I use so much of both herbs. Lavender, hyssop and rosemary make particularly delightful low hedges in a herb

garden, either left to grow freely or trimmed to shape. In a town garden, decorative tiles or even scallop shells can make an attractive frame to each border. It is still possible to find the dark grey scroll-edge Victorian garden tiles in demolition yards – otherwise reproduction ones can also be easily obtained.

Before you choose which herbs to grow, find out what kind of soil you have and whether it has good or poor drainage. Refer to the cultivation charts on pages 218–219 to check ideal growing conditions. Unless you have naturally well-drained ground it may be necessary to excavate the garden area, lay agricultural drainage pipes and replace the topsoil with a mixture of gritty sand and loam. In their natural habitat, Mediterranean herbs love dry, parched conditions, so, on heavy clay soils, I find raised beds or low stone walls with drainage holes provide an ideal environment for these herbs.

After you have considered all these points and are ready to transfer your herb garden design to the site, first of all pace it out to make sure that it fits the space. Use string and wooden pegs driven into the ground, or a hose-pipe, pebbles or bricks to mark out the design before you start to dig, so that, if need be, you can make alterations at this early stage. To mark out a circular bed, secure a string to a post in the centre of the bed, measure its radius along the string, and at this point tie a bottle filled with fine sand to the post. Then, keeping the string taut, drag the bottle along the ground to mark out the circle with a line of sand.

Every herb garden benefits from having a focal point such as a sundial, a garden statue or a magnificent urn or jardinière. The imposing marble bowl resting on three lions in the centre of the herb garden at Sissinghurst is a particularly splendid example. Alternatively, if you have room, a deciduous tree like a mulberry, *Morus nigra*, or a fringe tree, *Chionanthus virginicus*, planted in the right place, can provide a beautiful pivot to the garden. Depending on the tree you choose, consider also planting a fragrant old-fashioned rambling rose to climb through its branches, such as the beautiful creamy-white 'Kiftsgate', or pure white 'Rambling Rector'. If you can, install or plant such a feature as soon as you start your construction work, then the herbs will grow naturally around it and add a timeless look to the garden.

ABOVE *Enclosing walls and hedges help to create a special atmosphere, making the herb garden feel like a world apart. More practically, they also provide shelter for tender species and surfaces for climbers to cling to. For hedging, rosemary, hyssop and lavender all make good alternatives to box.*

LEFT *However informal the planting is to be, every herb garden benefits from having a focal point of some sort. In the gorgeous grey garden at Lambrook Manor in Somerset, paths diverge and plants cluster around the base of a beautifully weathered bird bath, which makes a subtle centre piece.*

ABOVE *Paths merit more thought than they often receive, not only from the aesthetic point of view but also because the material you choose will have important implications for both cost and maintenance. Here the edges of a brick path are softened, if not completely hidden, by an emphatic planting of chives.*

PLANTING

Colour is one of the most important factors in setting the mood in any garden. It may be a deciding factor in your choice of plants, and it will also affect the way you group them. The muted palette of silver, soft pink and mauve shown here will tend to create an atmosphere of soothing tranquillity.

Choosing which herbs to plant in your garden is a pleasurable task and, above all, a matter of personal choice. On the whole, a cook will prefer to grow culinary herbs, whereas somebody wanting to make pot-pourri will choose aromatic plants and so on.

Whatever your needs it is useful to bear in mind that the most successful plantings have a harmony of shade and shape. To me every garden, every border has a mood depending upon its design and its choice of plants. Gertrude Jekyll described planting as 'painting a landscape with living things' and it holds this kind of magic for me, too.

Foliage colour is one of the most effective ways of achieving the mood or 'landscape' you desire. For example, if you want a quiet, restful garden, select herbs with muted, grey-green and blue-green leaves. Why not recreate the lovely combination of white roses and silver-grey rosemary bushes favoured by the Duke of Bedford in his Royal garden in Paris. In complete contrast, a jolly, showy midsummer herb garden would contain yellow-green herbs like tansy, golden marjoram and feverfew as well as lots of bright yellow and orange marigolds and nasturtiums. For a serene and peaceful effect during early summer, borrow one of Miss Jekyll's happiest planting schemes by growing hostas and scented violets at the foot of heavily perfumed Madonna lilies, and provide a backdrop of dark green, glossy bay trees, clipped to make a hedge.

To achieve the most harmonious and natural look possible, it pays to consider the shape of each plant. The gardening writer Christopher Lloyd talks in terms of 'buns and cones', which I find helpful when planning new planting schemes. The garden can look dull unless you vary the shape and leaf colour of adjacent plants. The feathery grey spikes of the curry plant look well when placed next to red sage and clumps of clove pinks for example.

First of all, decide where to plant the trees and shrubs in your herb garden as these are going to stay in position for some time and may reach a considerable size. Though I might have planned the position on paper I double-check before planting a bay tree or juniper bush by fixing a stake in the ground to get some idea of how the full-grown herb will look. Unless you trim it to shape, a bay tree can grow very large – up to 6m (19½ft) high and as much around – and a tall variety of rosemary can reach from 1 to 2m (3¼ to 6½ft) if left to grow unchecked.

Next, plan the positions of the medium and small perennial herbs, bearing in mind that herbs like thyme, marjoram and hyssop do spread and are best planted not too close to the edge of a border unless you intend to trim them to shape. Allow 20–30cm (8–12in) between the plants. Once established, some herbs such as borage, fennel and chives seed themselves so readily that they need to be thinned in the spring.

Finally, once all danger of frost has passed, the annual herbs and edible flowers can be sown or planted in position.

Tender specimens, such as scented-leaved geraniums, are best planted in pots. Either transplant them to an antique urn or an attractive jardinière and position them where it is easy to brush your hands over their leaves as you pass, so they perfume the air. Alternatively, simply leave the plants in their pots and sink them into the ground up to their rims so that they can be returned quite easily to a frost-proof place at the end of the summer.

An established and successfully planted herb garden has a rich and varied appearance with little or no soil visible. Newly planted herbs soon spread out to cover most of the ground, however, and any remaining bare soil can be given a mulch of peat mixed with sand, wood bark or even gravel – this not only suppresses the weeds but gives the herb garden a neat and attractive look.

For those people who are fortunate enough to have large gardens, where space is not a problem, bold, impressionistic splashes of colour can have a quite spectacular and dazzling visual effect, as with these interlocking drifts of the common and golden form of marjoram covering a bank.

CREATING
A PAVED HERB GARDEN

A paved garden, having its origin in the brick and tiled courtyard gardens of early Islamic culture, has an aesthetically pleasing formality. The smooth surfaces of stone, tiles or brick that reflect both light and heat make an admirable setting for a wide variety of hardy perennial herbs.

The air of ordered calm that paving contributes to a garden, allied to the low maintenance that it requires, makes a paved garden eminently suitable for a town house. Some particularly fine examples are to be found in Paris, London and Madrid where they are distinguished by the high quality and originality of their design and imaginative choice of plants.

On the whole, a paved herb garden works best on a fairly small scale. It might be enclosed like a courtyard, or it could be surrounded with an informal hedge – perhaps of shrub roses or rosemary. However, a paved herb garden with a good strong design can also work well when placed in an open situation and set in an expanse of gravel or lawn.

One of the best positions for a paved herb garden is where it adjoins the house. Here the all-weather surface provides an ideal setting for your favourite herbs and also the perfect site for an outdoor room. To allow space for garden furniture and for sitting, drinking and eating it's advisable to design the paved garden so that the herbs frame the space rather than obstruct it. The herb borders can be at ground level or slightly higher, in a raised bed set behind a low brick or stone wall. In a woodland garden raised beds tend to look more in keeping with the landscape when surrounded by tree off-cuts, peat blocks or weathered railway sleepers.

The paved bee-skep herb garden at the American Museum at Claverton Manor near Bath is well sited, close enough to the house to be used often. The small, square garden is built at the sunny, sheltered end of the main terrace that stretches along the back of the house. The central circular border holds an old-fashioned straw bee-skep, and flowering herbs such as melissa, bee-balm and lavender, that are always visited by bees, are planted in the box-hedged beds around it.

As an alternative to a rectangle or square herb terrace, a semi-circle forms a good strong garden design. Constructed with the straight side against the house – its doors and windows opening onto it – the pattern is properly exploited by making wedge-shaped beds of herbs resemble the spokes of a wheel radiating from the centre.

Traditional geometric patterns, like a chequerboard or wheel, work well in the garden when paved with bricks or stone sets. It is important,

Neat and stylish, a paved garden combines minimum maintenance with an air of ordered calm. Here, the simple design of the sundial and birdbath complements this style.

though, to use a paving material that is sympathetic to the design of the garden and the character of nearby buildings.

The variety of materials available is wide: stone flags and bricks in different colours and patterns are traditional choices, but slate, quarry tiles or even ceramic ones, wood, granite sets, cobbles and pebbles are all possible alternatives. A little judicious mixing can be successful too: patterns of cobbles or pebbles, for instance, can look attractive if let into bricks or granite sets. If you use them to make a path, however, lay them with care so that they are comfortable to walk on. And whatever you are using, try to make sure that the surface the path is to be laid on is as level as possible.

Costs also vary enormously, but as the area of most herb gardens is small and having the right colour and texture of the paving is so crucial, it may be tempting to splash out a little. Old or second-hand materials, if you are lucky enough to find them, have the double advantage of keeping costs down and looking beautifully weathered immediately. But any hard surfaces – even utilitarian concrete – can be mellowed and made more friendly-looking by careful planting. Tufts and cushions of creeping herbs such as thyme and pennyroyal will quickly soften edges and fill crevices, as well as releasing their heady, aromatic fragrance as you crush their leaves underfoot.

On the whole it is wisest, and also often most practical, to choose materials that will complement the house. Sometimes paving can exactly match the fabric of an adjacent building. Years ago I lived in a small red-brick cottage in the Thames Valley. The house took its name from the fine herringbone pattern of brickwork in its walls. From the wooden picket gate on the road, a smooth moss-encrusted brick path led up to the front door which was flanked by a large rosemary bush and a clump of silver-grey lavender. The path had been cleverly converted into a long narrow herb garden by planting pockets of herbs in the crevices between the bricks. Low, creeping herbs such as woolly thyme, Corsican thyme, chamomile and pennyroyal made small puffy cushions along its length. Taller herbs such as rue and lavender, santolina and marjoram were planted in narrow borders on each side of the path. The more tender herbs, tarragon and basil, grew in old

terracotta pots so that they could be overwintered under the wide porch.

The paved herb garden opposite has a strong practical appeal. The overall size is about 6 × 4m (19½ × 13ft) although, if space is at a premium, just half the design could be planted and would work equally well.

The framework of paths gives the garden a formal aspect that is softened by the clumps of herbs spreading over their edges. Stone paving slabs, measuring 46cm (18in) square, and frost-proof stock bricks are laid on a dryish mortar mix foundation, with the bricks grouped in blocks of three – two in one direction and the third laid lengthways across them. The pattern is reversed for the next block, and so on.

The garden is set in level lawn a fraction higher than the paving so that the grass can be mown straight over it, thereby saving time on edge trimming. The open position gives a light, airy feel to the design and one of its charms is that within a short time it looks well established and mature. The herbs, with their many different shapes and colours, create a beautiful display which is complemented by the textures and tones of the red brick and weathered stone paths.

Making clever use of limited space, this design manages to accommodate a good selection of common culinary herbs while at the same time keeping them accessible from the all-weather paved paths. A strongly symmetrical plan such as this can even be subdivided: for a more compact garden half the design could stand on its own, remembering to keep the central bay tree in order to provide a vertical accent.

PAVED HERB GARDEN

1 **SAGE,** *Salvia officinalis*
2 **SOUTHERNWOOD,** *Artemisia abrotanum*
3 **BISTORT,** *Persicaria bistorta*
4 **FOXGLOVE,** *Digitalis purpurea*
5 **CLOVE PINK,** *Dianthus caryophyllus*
6 **ROSA MUNDI,** *Rosa gallica* 'Versicolor'
7 **BAY,** *Laurus nobilis*
8 **POT MARJORAM,** *Origanum onites*
9 **PARSLEY,** *Petroselinum crispum*
10 **SILVER POSIE,** *Thymus repandia* 'Silver Posie'
11 **GARDEN ORACH,** *Atriplex hortensis*
12 **ALLIUM,** *Allium*
13 **PURPLE TOADFLAX,** *Linaria purpurea*
14 **LAVENDER,** *Lavandula angustifolia*
15 **MARJORAM,** *Origanum vulgare*
16 **MUSK MALLOW,** *Malva moschata*
17 **PURPLE SAGE,** *Salvia officinalis* 'Purpurascens'
18 **WALL GERMANDER,** *Teucrium chamaedrys*
19 **ROSA MUNDI,** *Rosa gallica* 'Versicolor'
20 **GERANIUM,** *Geranium macrorrhizum roseum*
21 **APPLE MINT,** *Mentha sauveolens*
22 **PEPPERMINT,** *Mentha X piperita*

CREATING A
CULINARY HERB GARDEN

To a gardening cook the deliberations about the style and location of a herb garden have more than just horticultural or aesthetic significance. On the whole, the best culinary herb garden is practical, inspiring and sited as near as possible to the kitchen. That said, clearly not every kitchen door opens onto the ideal spot for growing herbs. So, as with cooking itself, you may need to be ingenious and resourceful.

It is surprising, though, how often an unpromising corner of the garden can be transformed into a delightful herb garden provided that you can come up with the right design.

Even if your starting point is a sunless backyard, there is usually a solution to be found, given a modicum of imagination and flair. In this instance, why not paint the walls white and create a *trompe-l'oeil* effect by affixing large sheets of mirror glass to reflect all available light, then framing it with grey-painted trellis and shine carefully installed outdoor grow-lights onto the plants to promote vigorous, healthy growth.

If, however, you have more space at your disposal, your scope for designing the perfect cook's garden is limitless. The history of herb garden design illustrates the vast number of possible arrangements that work well for culinary herbs. Perhaps a medieval *herbarium* with a series of rectangular beds each assigned to a different herb is appealing, or a *parterre anglais*, planted with your favourite cooking herbs, each bed neatly corralled with box hedging. Or then again, an attractive Elizabethan herb garden might be your choice, with its rich medley of herbs and scented flowers.

The beautiful culinary herb garden opposite has been created in the sheltered, walled orchard of a house in Wiltshire.

One's first impression is of generous abundance: large verdant clumps of lemon balm jostle with mounds of chives and marjoram, a cloud of old-fashioned roses in full bloom is glimpsed through a colonnade of gauzy fennel, and rows of garden peas, French beans and onions fill in the gaps, in the style of a *jardin potager*.

The herbs are cultivated in large, triangular borders almost like a crop – and I imagine that there is enough of each one to satisfy even the most demanding cook. A further advantage of this attractive design is that you can quite easily develop a similar style in an existing kitchen garden either by gradually replacing vegetable plants with herbs or by colonizing unused space.

Once you've decided on the position and size of your herb garden, it is sensible to think next about its principal directions or axes, and, also,

A glorious cornucopia of herbs, vegetables and old-fashioned flowers fills this potager *to the brim. The planting scheme is complex but the garden is both attractive and space-saving.*

the focal point of the design. In the Wiltshire garden, the framework of diagonal grass paths intersects at an open square in the centre of the garden, to make a clearing large enough for a seat or a table. At the widest point of each border a young standard apple tree has been planted to maintain the continuity of the old orchard. A wigwam of beansticks makes an ideal support for a rambling golden hop or trailing nasturtiums. Like the trees, it provides another vertical feature to balance the high stone wall that stands at the back of the garden.

The unobstructed, well-drained paths are a boon to a cook in a hurry or during a downpour. Wide borders may need firm, level stepping stones set among the plants so that you can gather the herbs without trampling on the soil. Alternatively, you can extend the path into the border by making a series of bays or inlets so that you can reach the herbs easily. And why not place a wooden seat or a stone figure in one or more of the bays to add interest to the garden?

To some people a culinary herb garden may appear simply functional – just a way of producing fresh herbs for the kitchen. Yet every good cook knows how a beautiful garden inspires one's cooking and leads to fresh gastronomic ideas. Then, gathering home-grown herbs becomes one of the most pleasurable preludes to a fine meal.

For me, the most outstanding culinary herb garden of the past flourished during the sixteenth century; a present-day Elizabethan herb garden is not only a place of dazzling beauty but an unending source of inspiration. The Elizabethan fondness for flowers which was eloquently expressed in the paintings, fabrics and tapestries of the time sprang from their enthusiasm for the garden, where they grew flowers for pleasure and for medicinal, cosmetic and culinary purposes.

In my own herb garden I plant both annual and perennial edible flowers. Neat cushions of grey-leaved, pink-flowered dianthus grow next to the shaggy-headed bee-balm, blue cornflowers and heavy-scented stocks. Some of these flowers make a charming last-minute addition to a salad or a cool, sweet custard. Others I use as a garnish for a plate or a tray of food. Over the years I have compiled a list of flowers that are safe to eat. Some, such as violets, rose petals and marigolds have a delightful and unique taste, whereas the

flowers of herbs such as rosemary and lavender usually have a delicate flavour of the herb itself. Edible herb flowers are listed below:

EDIBLE HERB FLOWERS
Basil, bay, bergamot, borage, chamomile, chervil, chive, claytonia, dill, elderflower, fennel, hyssop, lavender, lemon balm, lemon verbena, lovage, marjoram, mint, pineapple sage, purslane, rocket, rosemary, sage, salad burnet, sorrel, sweet cicely, sweet woodruff, tarragon, tansy, thyme.

PLANTS WITH EDIBLE FLOWERS
Allysum, anchusa, begonia, carnation, chrysanthemum, clover, coleus, cornflower, cosmos, cottage pink, cowslip, dahlia, day-lily, dianthus, forget-me-knot, geranium, gladioli, hawthorn blossom, hibiscus, hollyhock, honeysuckle, hop, jasmine, lilac, lime, mallow, marigold, mesembryanthemum, monarda, nasturtium, heart's-ease pansy, rose, sedum, stock, tiger lily, violet, zonal pelargonium.

As any cook knows, the best culinary herb gardens are not merely functional but also inspirational. Of course they must be practical, for there is no point in growing a mouthwatering range of herbs if you then cannot reach them to gather a few sprigs, but they must also tempt you on to new gastronomic delights. In this garden generous and relaxed abundance is the keynote.

A SCENTED AND CULINARY HERB GARDEN

1 **COMFREY,** *Symphytum officinale*
2 **SUNFLOWER,** *Helianthus annuus*
3 **POPPY,** *Papaver*
4 **TANSY,** *Tanacetum vulgare*
5 **SCOTS LOVAGE,** *Ligusticum scoticum*
6 **SWEET CICELY,** *Myrrhis odorata*
7 **ANGELICA,** *Angelica archangelica*
8 **ROSEMARY,** *Rosmarinus officinalis*
9 **EVENING PRIMROSE,** *Oenothera biennis*
10 **ELECAMPANE,** *Inula helenium*
11 **WOAD,** *Isatis tinctoria*
12 **DILL,** *Anethum graveolens*
13 **VALERIAN,** *Valeriana officinalis*
14 **ALKANET,** *Anchusa officinalis*
15 **BERGAMOT,** *Monarda didyma*
16 **SAGE,** *Salvia officinalis*
17 **LAVENDER,** *Lavandula angustifolia*
18 **MARJORAM,** *Origanum vulgare*
19 **CLARY SAGE,** *Salvia sclarea*
20 **ROSEMARY,** *Rosmarinus officinalis*
    COTTON LAVENDER, *Santolina chamaecyparissus*
21 **CORNFLOWER,** *Centaurea cyanus*
22 **CARAWAY,** *Carum carvi*
23 **CORIANDER,** *Coriandrum sativum*
24 **WINTER SAVORY,** *Satureja montana*
25 **WHITE HYSSOP,** *Hyssopus officinalis* 'Albus'
26 **SUMMER SAVORY,** *Satureja hortensis*
27 **COMMON MINT,** *Mentha spicata*
28 **PARSLEY,** *Petroselinum crispum*
29 **GARDEN THYME,** *Thymus vulgaris*
30 **ENGLISH MACE,** *Achillea decolorans*
31 **ANISE HYSSOP,** *Agastache anethiodora*
32 **CHIVES,** *Allium schoenoprasum*
33 **BUCKLER-LEAFED SORREL,** *Rumex scutatus*
34 **SALAD BURNET,** *Sanguisorba minor*
35 **OREGANO,** *Origanum vulgare*
36 **HORSERADISH,** *Armoracia rusticana*
37 **TARRAGON,** *Artemisia dracunculus*
38 **BRONZE FENNEL,** *Foeniculum vulgare* 'Purpurascens'
39 **WELSH ONION,** *Allium fistulosum*

CREATING A SMALL FORMAL HERB GARDEN

Many gardeners with a sense of history are attracted to the idea of recreating a garden style from the past. The formal garden which most immediately evokes the past is the knot garden. This pattern of interweaving plants exerts an almost hypnotic charm, as you allow your eyes to follow the intricate paths of the plants, curving and looping like an unfurled ribbon.

A knot garden, though, is definitely not for the impatient: it takes time to establish and then requires the continual care of weeding and clipping to maintain its pristine beauty. The Connecticut knot garden overleaf measures 3.5m (12ft) square and its symmetrical pattern is composed of two squares, a circle and a continuous four-loop knot.

Blue-grey-leaved thrift with its rose-pink flowers forms the outer square, with the knot garden favourite, wall germander, planted in the inner square. The circle is planted with common rue and the knot ribbon is defined with the 'Blue Mound' variety of the same herb. Ground-hugging woolly thyme frames each corner of the garden while clumps of silver-leaved lamb's ears and glaucous-blue circle onion fill the spaces inside the smaller square.

To achieve the authentic tapestry-like effect, the planting must adhere to the pattern of the knot. In this case the line of rue 'Blue Mound' crosses over the squares of thrift and germander as it travels out from the centre, but passes under them as it returns. Accordingly, the garden achieves a rhythm and movement that is most engaging. Like its Tudor forebears, the garden has been designed to be viewed from above or from the first-floor window of the owner's house.

In summer the varied shades of green and blue herbs set against a background of white gravel define its pattern. In winter, in this all-weather garden, a layer of powdery snow reveals the pattern of the knot just as clearly.

From the knot garden an arbour of pleached Seckel pears leads to a second, slightly larger formal garden – this time based on a Renaissance style and ornamented with an antique sundial.

The symmetry of this rectangular garden is achieved by means of a pattern of raised beds separated by grey brick paths. The central circular border is carpeted with the felty leaves of lamb's ears and studded with mounds of *Artemisia schmidtiana* and creeping lemon thyme. Above it the sundial is placed on a weathered terracotta plinth. This vertical focal point is echoed by four white stone jardinières that flank both entrances to the garden. The silver theme is underscored by the *Helichrysum petiolare* with its trailing growth.

A pair of mop-head standard junipers flanks this delightful exercise in domestic-scale formality. The combination of square, stone plant pots creates a symmetrical order.

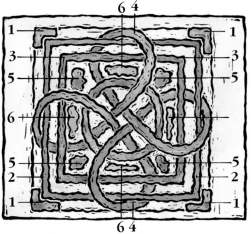

The swooping curves and labyrinthine interlocking lines of this Renaissance knot garden in miniature are almost mesmerizing in their charm. Subtle gradations of colour and texture add to the complexity, requiring meticulous care in planting and equally painstaking maintenance.

Dwarf hedges define the L-shaped beds of herbs, and dark green prisms and spheres of close-clipped box are a reminder of the topiary of the Renaissance garden. Wooden benches, each shaded by a trellis arbour, offer a welcome retreat during the heat of the day and emphasize the feeling of an outdoor room. At one side, two fine mop-head standard junipers highlight the domestic scale of this delightful herb garden.

Aspiring herb gardeners who are looking for ideas will be able to learn quite a lot from both the American gardens on this page. One aspect that is important yet is easily overlooked is the scale of both gardens – neither is very big and either would fit comfortably into the average size plot. Even a small city garden could accommodate the simple and compact knot design.

Generally, in a small formal herb garden the number of different herbs is deliberately restricted. This restraint extends to the range of surfaces that the garden utilizes – it is characteristic of a formal herb garden that less is more. Although it might appear easier to design a garden with less in it, it usually proves more of a challenge, because the most successful result depends upon every element working perfectly – both separately and together – and there is little room for mistakes. For this reason, careful deliberation is needed before you actually start to construct the garden.

First of all, it is necessary to decide on the landscape of the garden. Should it be predominantly soft and leafy with plenty of plants? Or would you prefer a more organized and ordered appearance, where the fixed elements of paths, paving, walls and steps are well emphasized? Perhaps the idea of making the plants themselves the formal element, by means of trimmed box hedging and clipped topiary, answers your needs.

Gardeners of the past have dealt with questions like these in a rich variety of ways. At Castle Drogo in Devon, the problem of how to make the gravel path that leads down from the herb terraces more interesting has been solved by breaking the straight edge of the path with a series of semi-circles, arranged in pairs opposite each other, each a mirror image so that the border narrows on one side of the path as it widens on the other. It's the kind of clever, unobtrusive solution typical of the best garden design.

In Italy, I discovered a charming formal herb garden that had been built at the foot of a high stone wall. To overcome the dwarfing effect of the wall, a series of garden statues each set on a stone column were arranged alternatively with narrow, clipped juniper bushes along the main paths of the garden. These acted as a visual bridge between the height of the wall and the low carpet of herbs at ground level. The idea could easily be adapted, on a simpler scale, by using tall pots instead.

To many of us, there is an air of peace and balance in the formal herb garden that is most seductive. With its classical symmetry and its atmosphere of intimacy and seclusion, it can be scaled down to fit even the tiniest pocket handkerchief of a garden. In a world of increased pressure a small formal herb garden can become a heavenly oasis.

KNOT GARDEN

1 **WOOLLY THYME,** *Thymus pseudolanuginosus*
2 **THRIFT,** *Armeria maritima*
3 **GERMANDER,** *Teucrium chamaedrys*
4 **'BLUE MOUND' RUE,** *Ruta graveolens* 'Jackman's Blue'
5 **LAMB'S EAR,** *Stachys byzantina*
6 **CIRCLE ONION,** *Allium senescens* var. *glaucum*

SMALL FORMAL HERB GARDEN

1 **LAMB'S EAR,** *Stachys byzantina*
2 **SILVER MOUND,** *Artemisia schmidtiana*
3 **'SECKLE' PEAR TREES**
4 **GOLDEN SAGE,** *Salvia officinalis* 'Aurea' (in containers)
   WOOLLY THYME, *Thymus pseudolanuginosus* (in containers)
5 **DWARF BOXWOOD,** *Buxus sempervirens* 'Suffruticosa'
6 **BOX,** *Buxus sempervirens*
7 **HIBISCUS,** *Hibiscus syriacus* (pots sunken into ground, taken indoors in winter)
8 **CAMPHOR SC. SOUTHERNWOOD,** *Artemisia abrotanum* var. *camphorata*
9 **LAVENDERS,** *Lavandula angustifolia* 'Munstead'; *L.a* 'Hidcote'; *L. x intermedia* 'Vera'
10 **JUNIPERS,** *Juniper virginicina*
11 **BURNET,** *Sanguisorba canadensis*
12 **CATNIP,** *Nepeta cataria*
13 **FENNEL,** *Foeniculum vulgare*

14 **COMMON HOREHOUND,** *Marrubium vulgare*

15 **COSTMARY,** *Tanacetum balsamita*

16 **AMORISIA,** *Chenopodium botrys*

17 **AMERICAN NARROW-LEAVED MOUNTAIN MINT,** *Pycnanthemum pilosum*

18 **TARRAGON,** *Artemisia dracunculus*

19 **GOOD KING HENRY,** *Chenopodium bonus-henricus*

20 **MARJORAM,** *Origanum vulgare*

21 **MOTHERWORT,** *Leonurus cardiaca*

22 **SILVERLEAF HOREHOUND,** *Marrubium incanum*

23 **PINEAPPLE MINT,** *Mentha suaveolens* 'variegata'

24 **RUSSIAN SAGE,** *Perovskia atriplicifolia*

25 **AGRIMONY,** *Agrimonia eupatoria*

26 **MOONSHINE YARROW,** *Achillea* 'Moonshine'

27 **GAY FEATHER,** *Liatris spicata*

28 **YARROW,** *Achillea millefolium*

29 **HEMP AGRIMONY,** *Eupatorium cannabinum*

30 **LEMON BALM,** *Melissa officinalis*

31 **DYER'S BROOM,** *Genista tinctoria*

32 **GOLDEN SAGE,** *Salvia officinalis* 'Aurea'

33 **TRICOLOR SAGE,** *Salvia officinalis* 'Tricolor'

34 **PURPLE LEAF SAGE,** *Salvia officinalis* 'Purpurascens'

35 **YELLOW FOXGLOVE,** *Digitalis grandiflora*

36 **MEADOW CLARY,** *Salvia pratensis*

37 **VALERIAN,** *Centranthus ruber*

38 **BETONY,** *Stachys officinalis*

39 **LEMON THYME,** *Thymus* × *citriodorus*

A plan inspired by the designs of the sixteenth century, cool and classical yet full of romantic period charm. This herb garden is surprisingly practical too, as the brick paths between the beds provide handy access to the herbs themselves.

CREATING A SCENTED HERB GARDEN

A scented garden is the most romantic form of herb garden and one with a long and historic pedigree. In the medieval world fragrance was accorded a mystical spiritual quality akin to the power of music. The authority of the Bible, especially of course the intoxicating litany of perfumes which opens the *Song of Songs*, was quoted in support of the medieval belief that fragrance was a higher form of beauty. In the medieval and Renaissance world it must all too often have seemed an unattainable form of beauty, too: smells of all sorts would have assaulted the nose, but few of them would have been pleasant. Scented leaves and petals – used for strewing floors and for making garlands and pot-pourris, pillows and sachets, lotions and perfumes – were the only means available to most people for sweetening the air around them, and were treasured as such. Imagine, then, what a place of delight a scented garden would have been, with aromatic thyme and sweet woodruff underfoot, borders full of roses, pinks and lavender, a chamomile seat flanked by hyssop and rosemary, and perhaps a bower of jasmine and honeysuckle overhead. This is the legacy that we have inherited, which even now seems to endow the idea of a scented herb with a special and elusive magic.

And yet there is no secret to creating a garden like this, nor is it difficult. In fact people who have existing gardens often find it quite simple to convert to this style of garden since established borders, walls, arches and walks can be utilized by replacing non-scented plants with alternative fragrant varieties and well-chosen aromatic herbs.

In the delightful garden opposite, the designer has created a perfumed and pleasing environment composed of several smaller elements. This is an ambitious garden with over 50 herbs artfully arranged to form colour harmonies and precise architectural effects.

Although originally intended to fill a space of 18.25 × 15.25m (60 × 50ft), the asymmetric design could be adapted to a smaller space by laying out just part of the scheme. The design also provides an excellent blueprint for the gardener who wants to grow herbs in raised beds, a style of garden especially appreciated by the elderly, the wheelchair-bound and the blind.

A low, dwarf box hedge almost surrounds the focal point of the garden – a stone sundial. Four small gardens bounded by the box hedge each have a colour theme. The pink-flowered border, for instance, contains wall germander, soapwort, gravel root and cottage pinks. The three other borders contribute white, yellow and purple

A rustic bench invites you to linger among the heady fragrances of catmint and thyme. The location and style of the seat have been selected at an early stage of garden planning.

themes. Anyone unfamiliar with these versatile plants would be surprised that every single plant in this garden is a herb.

The all-pervading scents will attract dozens of bees and butterflies, and a cat will adore the 15.25m (50ft) border of catmint, which displays to advantage this glorious herb. The rustic bench placed among the riot of purple-blue blooms faces a cushioned bed of highly aromatic varieties of flowering thyme.

Culinary herbs are easy to gather from a charming U-shaped border that follows one of the boundaries, while beds of old-fashioned roses encircled with lavender and santolina form two islands of perfume at the side.

The gravel paths, laid over compacted hardcore, make a quick-draining surface. To provide an extra variation of height, some of the tender herbs, like pineapple sage and scented-leaved geraniums, might be grown in pots that stand directly on the gravel. Large, grand pots make an interesting feature and change of texture in a herb garden, and flowering herbs add splashes of colour. Of course, in some circumstances – where a garden is entirely gravelled or paved – a gardener may decide to grow all the herbs in pots (for more detailed advice on creating a container herb garden, see pages 60–63).

A scented herb garden is intended for lingering in – it should be so deliciously fragrant that you should find it impossible to drag yourself away from it. Pretty effects can be achieved by growing the plants at several different levels, from lavender in low beds, to basil in old terracotta pots and jasmine and honeysuckle creeping over trellises. I am particularly fond of the rose arbour herb garden that I designed in this way for a friend. It comprises a colour scheme of pale pinks, white and grey. The scheme is easily adaptable to a variety of circumstances. Although based on a series of round-topped wooden trellis arches, these could as easily be made from metal painted white or black. The arches are placed next to each other to form a circle, a square or an octagon, large enough, ideally, to accommodate some chairs and a table for outdoor dining. The enclosed space can be paved with stone or bricks, although gravel or a chamomile lawn would work well too. A collection of favourite fragrant climbing roses, summer jasmine and honeysuckles are

planted at the base of each arch so that they can clothe the framework and entwine overhead. At the foot of each climbing plant a circular border is planted with herbs that have aromatic leaves, such as rosemary, lavender, southernwood and lemon verbena. Madonna lilies, pale pink cottage pinks and grey-leaved white single daisies are grown in lead-grey troughs and pots so that they can be moved around and grouped to catch the sun or to flank a seat. The garden was not only a joy to plan and establish but it should continue to give pleasure for many years.

A scented herb garden outside the back door thus offers delight and refreshment to all the senses. And for dedicated cooks it also offers a wide variety of culinary herbs, with the bonus, according to John Worlidge, who wrote these words in 1677, of having the ability to aid digestion: 'Endeavour to make the principle Entrance into your garden out of the best Room in your House, your Walks being places of divertisement after a sedentary repast. The Aromatick Odours they yield, pleasant refreshments after a gross diet, and such innocent Exercises the best digestive to weak Stomacks. And let your principle Walk extend itself as far as you can . . . adorned with the choicest Plants for Beauty and Scent, and that there may be a succession of them through the year, not without Flower pots, which grace the best of Gardens.'

Nothing can equal the nostalgic, evocative romance of a perfumed garden, where the air hangs heavy with scents both lingering and fleeting, always changing with the rhythm of the seasons and the day. This is a garden where one should be able to dawdle and take time to enjoy the beautiful aromas of the herbs. The pleasurable experience is enhanced by the carefully planned paths and borders. One can make a scented herb garden from an existing garden simply by replacing plants with fragrant varieties or aromatic herbs.

A SCENTED HERB GARDEN

1 **CATMINT,** *Nepeta cataria*
2 **THYME,** *Thymus* species
3 **ALPINE STRAWBERRY,** *Fragaria vesca*
4 **MARJORAM,** *Origanum vulgare*
5 **COMMON ELDER,** *Sambucus nigra*
6 **RED SAGE,** *Salvia officinalis* 'Purpurascens'
7 **PINKS,** *Dianthus*
8 **GRAVELROOT,** *Eupatorium purpureum*
9 **WALL GERMANDER,** *Teucrium chamaedrys*
10 **SOAPWORT,** *Saponaria officinalis*
11 **FRENCH ROSE,** *Rosa gallica*
12 **SANTOLINA,** *Santolina chamaecyparissus*
13 **ROSA MUNDI,** *Rosa gallica* 'Versicolor'
14 **GRAPPENHALL LAVENDER,** *Lavandula X intermedia* 'Grappenhall'
15 **PURPLE HYSSOP,** *Hyssopus officinalis*
16 **BRONZE FENNEL,** *Foeniculum vulgare* 'Purpurascens'
17 **COMMON BOX,** *Buxus sempervirens*
18 **WINTER SAVORY,** *Satureja montana*
19 **RUE,** *Ruta graveolens*
20 **GOLDEN ELDER,** *Sambucus nigra* 'Aurea'
21 **APPLEMINT,** *Mentha suaveolens*

22 **SILVER POSIE THYME,** *Thymus repandia* 'Silver Posie'
23 **FENNEL,** *Foeniculum vulgare*
24 **SALAD BURNET,** *Sanguisorba minor*
25 **COMMON SORREL,** *Rumex acetosa*
26 **MINT,** *Mentha species*
27 **FRENCH TARRAGON,** *Artemisia dracunculus* 'Sativa'
28 **PARSLEY,** *Petroselinum crispum*
29 **SAGE,** *Salvia officinalis*
30 **CHIVES,** *Allium schoenoprasum*
31 **ROSEMARY,** *Rosmarinus officinalis*
32 **CURRY PLANT,** *Helichrysum italicum*
33 **EVENING PRIMROSE,** *Oenothera biennis*
34 **JERUSALEM SAGE,** *Phlomis fruticosa*
35 **SAGE,** *Salvia glutinosa*
36 **ELECAMPANE,** *Inula helenium*
37 **WOOLLY YARROW,** *Achillea tomentosum*
38 **MULLEIN,** *Verbascum thapsus*
39 **DYER'S CHAMOMILE,** *Anthemis tinctoria*
40 **TANSY,** *Tanacetum vulgare*
41 **GOLD VARIEGATED SAGE,** *Salvia officinalis* 'Icterina'
42 **WORMWOOD,** *Artemisia absinthium*
43 **BLUE LAVENDER,** *Lavandula angustifolia* 'Hidcote'
44 **SOUTHERNWOOD,** *Artemisia abrotanum*
45 **MULLEIN,** *Verbascum thapus*
46 **ROCK HYSSOP,** *Hyssopus officinalis aristatus*
47 **WHITE LAVENDER,** *Lavandula angustifolia* 'Nana Alba'
48 **SWEET WOODRUFF,** *Galium odoratum*
49 **ANGLELICA,** *Angelica archangelica*
   SWEET CICELY, *Myrrhis odorata*
50 **SWEET ROCKET,** *Hesperis matronalis*
51 **SNEEZEWORT,** *Achillea ptarmica*
52 **SAGE,** *Salvia hispanica*
53 **PINK LAVENDER,** *Lavandula angustifolia* 'Hidcote Pink'
54 **ALECOST,** *Tanacetum balsamita*

CONTAINER HERB GARDENS

On the hillsides of Provence or Umbria, clumps of wild herbs growing in their natural habitat flourish in remarkably little soil. In my garden in the Ardèche I often transplant tussocks of wild thyme and mint and find them very difficult to dislodge from their home among the rocky outcrops. But after several strong tugs the herb eventually comes free and emerges with its dry, wiry roots denuded of soil. Once replanted in the damper, richer soil down near the house, the herbs often grow more lushly but rarely as aromatically. However, if planted in a clay pot and placed on a sun-baked terrace or windowsill, the wild thyme or mint regain their former vigour and scent – for pot-grown herbs invariably prosper.

A container herb garden not only looks delightful and is highly convenient, but also has the great charm of being created almost overnight. Once you've assembled the containers and your selection of herbs, planting up the most compatible partners is easy and enjoyable.

Just like larger herb gardens, container herb gardens are found in a variety of styles: a white-painted olive-oil can overflowing with flowering rosemary outside a Greek taverna, a clump of mint sprouting from an old china teapot on an English cottage windowsill or a series of neat wooden boxes of herbs in the garden of a Connecticut

Marrying herbs to the huge variety of containers available is a great source of instant pleasure and satisfaction.

containers. So, even if your budget does not allow for beautiful antique jardinières, there are inexpensive wooden tubs and reasonably priced terracotta urns widely available. Even cheap plastic pots can be improved by the addition of a thin coat of mortar or household filler tinted grey or green. Almost all porous pots can be aged by brushing them with rainwater, milk or yoghurt every few weeks until they develop a patina.

Among my favourite containers are clusters of ordinary clay flowerpots discovered in country markets and second-hand shops. And wooden fruit boxes stained with blue-grey wood dye and planted up with groups of herbs can make a useful and comprehensive herb garden.

Statuesque urns and jardinières, or a fine lead cistern or stone sink, can provide the necessary focal point in a garden. On a terrace of weathered stone, a softly romantic look can easily be achieved with an urn of blush pink dwarf roses, trailing scented-leaved geraniums, cottage pinks and grey-leaved santolina.

Some herb gardeners prefer the restrained formalism of topiary, such as clipped bay trees in tubs placed at the doorway of a town house. Other woody herbs such as rosemary and lavender can also be trained and clipped into mop-head shapes. On a windy site, it's a good idea to cover the growing medium with gravel or heavy pebbles to weigh down the container. Matching pots well planted and artfully positioned can achieve a dramatic and attractive effect. Containers of tall-growing herbs can form an attractive and informal screen in a garden.

The best growing medium for containers is a mixture of equal parts of gritty sand, loam and peat plus a dose of slow-release fertilizer, or use one of the proprietary blends of peat specially designed for pot-grown plants. Every container should have one or more drainage holes to prevent the plant getting waterlogged. I like to place a good layer of broken clay pots, or crocks, in the base of the container to help lower the centre of gravity and improve the drainage.

If a pot is large, place a length of perforated hose-pipe vertically in the middle of the pot so that you can water the plant through it. Surround the pipe with the growing medium and finally plant the herbs. A strawberry pot or tub, which looks charming planted up with different varieties

Pots and troughs of culinary herbs on a kitchen windowsill (above) not only look charming, but are also handy for cooking. Mint and strawberries planted in a hanging basket (below) make a pretty and quite delicious combination.

farmhouse all look charming because they are appropriate to their setting. It is important to consider carefully the style of your container herb garden, as well as the scale and proportion of each container, before you start.

Fortunately, interest in herb growing has encouraged potters, garden centres and nurseries to extend their range of interesting pots and

of thyme, is best planted as you fill it with the soil mixture. Make a layer of crocks in the base of the pot and wedge a length of perforated hose-pipe vertically in the centre, then cover the crocks with soil until level with the first opening in the side of the pot. Place the herb plant on the soil and gently push its leaves out through the hole, then spread out the roots and cover with soil, pressing it down gently to hold the plant in position. Now add more soil with a trowel until level with the next opening and plant another herb in the same way.

Hanging baskets are best lined with sphagnum moss to facilitate drainage and to cut down on weight. To fill a wire basket, place pieces of moist moss with their green tufty growth flat against the wire. Then half fill with the growing medium, place the plants in position and bed them in well with extra medium. If the soil in a newly planted container looks too bare, try covering it with bark

chippings or gravel, or even sow some mustard and cress which will germinate quickly and provide a green edible sward which can be cropped as the main herbs grow and spread.

Water the herbs as they require it, bearing in mind that leafy fleshy herbs such as basil prefer a damp soil while those from the Mediterranean such as rosemary like slightly arid conditions. Each time you water the pots, give them a good drenching. Hanging baskets tend to lose much more moisture than other containers. During the summer give fast-growing herbs an occasional feed of liquid organic fertilizer. Woody herbs, like hyssop, rosemary and lavender, should be pruned after flowering to ensure strong healthy growth for the following year. Trim herbs regularly to keep them in good shape and, if necessary, winter the tender perennial herbs such as tarragon and chives under cover in a light frost-proof place.

Containers are a good and inexpensive solution to problems such as a lack of space or sun. A salad bowl of oakleaf lettuce, mint, parsley, chives and other shade-tolerant herbs, for instance, will thrive in a sunless corner of your garden.

WINDOWSILL AND CONSERVATORY HERB GARDENS

Quite the easiest place to create an indoor herb garden is on a windowsill. Since one of the essential requirements of plant life is plenty of light, this is clearly an excellent location as long as you remember to turn the pots round regularly to ensure even growth. A south-facing window is admirably suited to pots of Mediterranean herbs like sage, thyme, myrtle and rosemary, though the leafy, moisture-loving herbs such as sorrel and chives may flag unless shaded during the hottest part of the day. Given a choice, I prefer a wooden windowsill rather than one of stone or tiles because the latter tend to chill the pots during cold weather. One solution is to place a plank of wood or other insulating material under the pots to keep the roots warm and promote growth. Since plants like to grow in groups it makes sense, and often looks more attractive, to plant your herbs in a trough or bowl to create an indoor windowbox. Remember that if you lower a blind or pull curtains across the window at night then the herbs would prefer to be with you in the warmth of the room rather than shut out in the chilly – and possibly drafty – space against the window.

When I lived in a studio-flat with a single, large south-facing window I created the maximum growing space by adding glass shelves to accommodate my windowsill herbs. I utilized every suitable nook and cranny by suspending some of the lighter pots of herbs from large hooks fixed along the lintel above the window. The green tracery of leaves filtered the light into the room and provided an attractive natural screen, making a conventional curtain unnecessary.

Windows that face in other directions than south are best suited to shade-loving herbs or those that scorch easily such as mints and chervil. In a location with poor-quality light consider fitting a couple of horticultural grow-bulbs above the plants to boost their growth.

The term conservatory was first used by John Evelyn at the beginning of the eighteenth century. In Victorian England, Sir Joseph Paxton revolutionized the design of glass buildings. A magnificent example is still to be seen at Chatsworth House, Derbyshire, the home of the Duke of Devonshire. Unlike the more strictly functional glasshouse, a conservatory is intended as an extension of the house, with doors and even windows opening into it. In Victorian conservatories, ferns, palms, aromatic plants and scented flowers were among the plants cultivated. If space permitted, some of these conservatories incorporated curved bays which housed additional seating. The ladies of the house traditionally took tea, read or embroidered in this light, airy space which must have been a welcome haven after the over-furnished drawing rooms of the time. It is hardly surprising that during the last decade, with the introduction of double glazing and more maintenance-free methods of construction, the conservatory has made a widespread reappearance in Britain as well as remaining popular in the United States.

Herbs and aromatic plants are a natural choice for a conservatory. Although it is perfectly easy to simply line up containers of your favourite plants, I think it is worth taking a little trouble to create a proper indoor herb garden. If there is enough space you could construct permanent raised beds of stone, brick or wood. An excellent idea for the back wall of a conservatory comes from my friend, the food writer Sri Owen. In order to grow many different herbs in a small space she has constructed a stepped raised bed by fixing one long plank of wood on its edge at ground level. The space behind is filled with growing compost and then a second plank is placed, edge-down, halfway across to make a narrower, deeper border against the wall.

Traditionally, the back wall of a conservatory has been used for growing highly-scented roses, climbing plants like plumbago with its panicles of heavenly blue flowers or the deservedly popular and intensely-fragrant summer jasmine.

The scented-leaf geranium was an immensely popular Victorian plant, large pots of rose-scented geraniums were used as room fresheners in drawing rooms and halls. I find that the best place to group these lovely plants – and other aromatic herbs – is at an entrance to the conservatory or in a porch.

Unless your conservatory is in continuous shade, it is wise to have blinds or shades fitted. Most conservatories produce a range of temperatures in different parts. Obviously, it is important to grow your plants in the most advantageous positions with, for example, pots of lavender and rosemary in the hotter, sunnier positions and parsley and chervil in the cooler, shadier areas. Many fragrant flowers such as lilies, jasmine and roses prefer to have their roots in shade while their blooms thrive best in the sun.

OPPOSITE AND ABOVE *Where space is at a premium, a single south-facing windowsill can contain enough herbs to satisfy most cooks. All the Mediterranean herbs will enjoy basking in direct sunlight, but those which are shy of direct sunlight, such as mint and chervil, will thrive in a shadier position. A strawberry planter packed with a variety of different herbs is a compact way of making the most of a windowsill, while an ingenious arrangement of pot-holders makes use of vertical as well as horizontal space. Arrangements like this are practical as well as economical, as plants enjoy being grouped together and thrive in each other's company.*

Unless you want to keep them for purely decorative effect, most herbs are best harvested for drying just before they come into flower, when their production of aromatic oils is at its peak. After flowering the plant concentrates on reproduction, and its energies are diverted to producing seeds. For the majority of herbs the longest day signals the plant's readiness for harvesting. Once cut, the herbs should be hung to dry in a warm and airy place away from direct sunlight. The herbs need to dry as quickly as possible in order to preserve their properties, but direct heat or sunlight will damage them.

HARVESTING AND PRESERVING HERBS

Every herb has a time of optimum growth when its leaves are highly aromatic and the plant is producing the maximum amount of essential oils. This is the moment that every prudent herb grower anticipates with pleasure, for herbs harvested at this time are in the peak of condition and in the best state for preserving for use later in the year.

It is best to harvest the majority of herbs just before they come into flower. After flowering, the plant concentrates on reproduction and its energies are diverted to producing seeds.

Some herbs flower once a year while others – such as chives – which flower early in the season, can usually be persuaded to produce a second crop of blooms by fairly severe pruning after the first flowering. Similarly, a burst of young tender leaves can be coaxed from herbs like lovage, angelica and chervil, by cutting down their stems by about two thirds in midsummer to promote new growth that has a better flavour for drying or preserving.

The best time of day to harvest herbs is during the morning on a dry day. Gather each herb separately to prevent cross flavours and cut complete stems rather than individual leaves. This helps to keep the herb fresh until you are able to preserve it. Place the herbs in a flat-bottomed basket or box, and in very hot weather, cover the container with a damp cloth.

The simplest method of drying is to make a bunch of each kind of herb and hang it upside down in a warm, airy, sunless place. Mediterranean herbs like rosemary, thyme and marjoram dry beautifully this way. The quicker the herb dries the better its colour and flavour. I usually hang herbs for drying from a beam in the kitchen but a wooden airing rack or a high shelf works equally well. I have found that an electric food dryer or an oven set on low with the door ajar can also give good results.

In central Europe where herbs are dried on a large scale for making tisanes and teas, leaves – such as mint – and flowers, for instance, lime and chamomile, are spread out on large muslin sheets tacked to horizontal frames in well-ventilated drying sheds. A small-scale domestic version can be constructed quite easily at home, even by stretching a net curtain over the legs of an upturned chair. It is essential with this method to provide a fast-moving current of dry air and to turn the herbs regularly to prevent any mildew or off-flavours from developing.

When the herb is paper-dry, it should be stored in an airtight container out of direct light. Leave the leaves attached to the stem and crush them just before use to prevent any loss of flavour.

Herb flowers for drying should be gathered particularly carefully to prevent damage to their petals. Long-stemmed flowers required for decoration can be dried on their stalks. In this case, the simplest method is to hang the blooms upside down, either separately or in loose bunches so that the flowers are not touching. Place in a well-ventilated, dust-free place, out of direct sunlight, in order to preserve the colour of the blooms. Flowers with short stems or no stems – and which may need wiring for decorative purposes – can be dried by supporting each bloom on fine chicken wire. Or use an upturned cardboard box – make a series of holes and thread the stems of the flowers into them until the flower head is resting on the flat surface.

An Elizabethan method of drying flowers is to place them stalk-down in a shallow box of fine, dry silver sand, a thin layer of extra sand is sprinkled over the petals and the box is left in a warm, dark place until the flowers are dry. A modern and more effective alternative to sand is silica gel crystals (obtainable from a chemist or flower-arranging shop). Use the finest grade of crystals spread over the bottom of a cardboard box, place the flowers, stem down, on top and sprinkle a fine layer of crystals over the petals. Leave in a dark, dry place for 2–4 days until the flowers are paper-dry. Carefully remove the blooms, shaking them free of the silica gel crystals.

The best-flavoured herb seeds are harvested after allowing them to ripen on the plant for as long as possible. This calls for careful judgement – if you leave coriander, dill, fennel or parsley seed for too long on the parent plant, the seeds will drop onto the ground before you have time to pick them. In a dry climate it is possible to cover the seed head with a paper bag tied securely around the stem and leave until the seeds rattle when you shake the bag. In a temperate climate it is usually safer to cut the seed head of the herb just as the seed colour starts to turn from green to pale brown. Place the whole head of seed in a roomy paper bag and hang in a warm, dry place for a few weeks until the seeds are dry. They will then separate and fall to the bottom of the bag.

In former centuries drying was virtually the only way of preserving the precious aromas of herbs through the winter. Even though other methods are now possible, such as freezing and microwaving, drying remains the easiest and most picturesque way of keeping herbs. Rosemary, thyme, marjoram and other Mediterranean herbs will dry beautifully if simply tied in bunches and hung upside down in the kitchen. The bunches should be kept small, otherwise there is a danger that the stems in the centre will stay damp and grow mouldy.

GUIDE TO PROPAGATION

When it comes to propagation, herbs are no different from other members of the plant kingdom in that they can be raised from seed or produced vegetatively by means of cuttings, layering or root division.

Whatever one's age, the thrill of growing plants from seed never diminishes. All of the annual herbs such as basil and rocket, and some of the biennial herbs such as angelica and smallage are best raised from seed in the spring.

Sow seed thinly by shaking it from a folded paper cone. In the case of very small seed, mix in a little fine sand. Sprinkle the seed on top of a pot or pan of slightly damp sowing compost. Sprinkle a thin layer of sifted compost over the seed and very gently tamp down with a piece of wood. Either place the pot in a propagating case or cover it with a layer of newspaper and a sheet of glass. Move the pot to a warm windowsill or to a staged plant stand in a greenhouse – a minimum night temperature of 18°C (65°F) is required – until germination takes place. At that point remove the covering and, if necessary, water sparingly.

When the seedlings have produced two true leaves prick them out by lifting a few at a time with a spatula, taking care not to dislodge the soil from their roots. Repot by planting 1–3 seedlings in a pot of compost and grow on until large enough to transplant to the herb garden.

Alternatively sow 2–4 seeds of the herb in small peat pots and leave to germinate in the same way. At the seedling stage remove the weaker ones and leave the stronger seedling to grow on until large enough to transplant with its ball of compost.

Some herbs such as French tarragon cannot be raised from seed. These are increased by cuttings taken from midsummer onwards. Select 7.5–10cm (3–4in) long tip cuttings from the plant, trim away the leaves from the lower half of the stem and dip the base into hormone rooting powder. Using a pencil or narrow dibber make a hole at the edge of a pot of cuttings compost, pop in the cutting and gently firm the compost around it. Place in a mist propagator or cover the pot with a roomy plastic bag with a few airholes punched in it, and leave in a light, warm place for 2–4 weeks until the cuttings have formed roots. Remove the bag and grow on for 2–4 weeks until the root system is strong enough to allow you to transplant the cutting to another pot. It can then be overwintered under glass. After hardening off in the following spring, plant in the herb garden in late spring or early summer. All the woody-stemmed herbs such as rosemary, bay, juniper and lavender can be grown from tip cuttings.

French tarragon can also be increased by root division. This is best carried out when the plant is dormant in late autumn or early spring. Gently dig up the herb and carefully separate some of the long straggly roots, select some with growing tips and cut off cleanly from the parent plant. Replant each root to the same depth in potting compost in pots or in sifted soil in the herb garden. In an exposed garden, cover the new plants with a glass or plastic cloche to give them protection from the wind. Most of the herbaceous herbs such as marjoram, oregano and thyme can be increased by root division.

Perhaps the easiest method of all for increasing your number of herb plants is to use layering. Any straggly herb, particularly the prostrate varieties of thyme, hyssop and summer jasmine, work well with this method. Choose a trailing and healthy-looking stem of the herb and gently stretch it out away from the parent plant. Place a small heap of sifted cuttings compost about halfway along the stem or sink a pot of the compost into the ground. Cover the stem with 2.5–5cm (1–2in) of compost and, if necessary, pin it down with a piece of bent wire. Leave for 6–8 weeks, or longer in cold weather, until fine roots have formed, then cut the new plant from the parent and transfer to permanent quarters. Layering can be done at any time during the growing season.

Happily some herbs propagate themselves with little help from the gardener. Among others, borage, angelica, fennel and clary sage, if allowed to form seedheads, will shed their seed on the ground around the parent plant. This seed germinates easily in warm, damp weather enabling the gardener simply to transplant the seedling herbs to their proper place in the herb garden when large enough to handle.

The prudent gardener saves seed of his favourite herbs in order to produce plants for his own garden or to give as gifts or to sell. The best time to collect herb seeds is just before the plant itself disperses them, usually in late summer. In this way, the seeds will be mature and well dried, by the air and the sun, and they should store well until needed for sowing. Cut off the seedhead and place it upside down in a paper bag. Tie up the open end and hang the bag in a warm, dry place for two weeks or longer. The seeds are ready to remove from the bag when they are dry enough to rattle when shaken. Sort out the seeds and discard the rest of the plant. Transfer the seeds to an airtight container, label and date it and store in a cool, dry, dark place until required for sowing.

Herb gardeners seem to be fecund creatures – forever producing seedlings and cuttings from their favoured plants. It is useful, if you have room, to set some space aside for a nursery bed in which to raise herb plants. This is also a good place to cosset that slip of pink-flowered rosemary or a cutting of yellow-leaved bay – given by a friend or snaffled from another garden, as keen gardeners are wont to do.

The nursery bed is the best place to grow stock plants from which you can take cuttings. A new formal herb garden, like a knot or a parterre, will require a large number of young hedging herbs when it is planted up. If you plan well ahead it is easy to produce all the plants yourself, which is not only considerably cheaper but also highly satisfying. Tip cuttings can be taken from all the herbs suitable for low hedging such as box, curry plant, hyssop, lavender, rue, santolina and wall germander.

Occasionally, the nursery bed has to become a hospital bed, where ailing plants are nursed back to health. When a herb fails to flourish, it may well be because it was planted in the wrong place – a Mediterranean herb, like rosemary, does not enjoy growing in a cold, damp situation and would prefer to bask in the sunshine with its roots in a light, well-drained soil, along with other heat-loving herbs such as catmint, lavender, santolina, nasturtium, rue and many others. Do not make the mistake either of thinking that you will be giving these plants a treat by enriching the soil: the majority of herbs with Mediterranean origins actually prefer poor soil, and over-manuring can result in abundant growth at the expense of scent and flavour.

Other herbs relish rich, moist conditions and are wretched in a sun-baked site: green, crisp-leaved sorrel, for example, or fragrant sweet violets, or pungent horseradish. In between there lies the whole spectrum of herbs, from those like sweet woodruff which like rich deep soil to others like valerian which will seed themselves in the tiniest crevice in a wall. The surest approach is to try and match the conditions in which any herb grows in the wild.

Since much of your success as a herb gardener depends on knowing what conditions each herb prefers, a checklist is helpful when making a planting plan for a new herb garden. Almost all herbs will grow well in full sun, though many are tolerant of a wide range of conditions and therefore appear in more than one category. See the herb directory on pages 70–91 for more information on herb cultivation.

HERB DIRECTORY

Allium sativum, **GARLIC**

Allium sativum
Liliaceae
GARLIC

CULTIVATION A hardy perennial, garlic has aromatic, narrow, green leaves and white flowers in its second summer of growth. It reaches 30–45cm (12–18in) and prefers well-drained, moderately fertile soil and full sun. Propagate it by planting the cloves of garlic in early spring or late autumn. Grow it as a companion plant in fruit and vegetable gardens to reduce aphid activity. Harvest it in late summer when the top growth has shrivelled, digging up the heads of garlic. Dry the heads outside for several days, then tie them in bundles or plaits and store in a cool, dry, dark place until needed. A useful garden, border and container herb.

USES Culinary, horticultural, medicinal
In a wide range of cuisines from all over the world, garlic is regarded as an essential flavouring. Its pervasive but delicious flavour is a natural partner to many meat, fish, vegetable, egg and cheese dishes. The herb is also cooked on its own to produce a mellow, less pungent-tasting form.

The medicinal claims for garlic are considerable. The herb contains a sulphide of the radical Allyl, which is antiseptic and therefore combats bacterial infections such as common colds. Garlic has also been recommended as a treatment for hypertension and rheumatism. The beneficial part of garlic is that which produces its very distinctive smell. Odourless garlic capsules do not work.

Allium schoenoprasum
Liliaceae
CHIVES

CULTIVATION This hardy perennial has aromatic, hollow, grass-like leaves and purple or white flowers from late spring. It grows to a height of 15–75cm (6–29in) and prefers fertile, well-drained soil and sun or light shade. Propagate it by sowing seeds or planting bulblets in spring or by dividing the plant in autumn, planting them 15–23cm (6–9in) apart. Harvest the leaves and flowers whenever they are available. It is an attractive garden, border, edging, container and conservatory herb. The essential oils in chives have anti-fungal and insecticide properties, so they can be used as companion plants for vegetables and fruit vulnerable to aphids.

USES Culinary, household
All members of the Allium *family provide essential ingredients for good cooking. The slim, cylindrical leaves of chives give a delicate onion flavour to a wide variety of dishes, such as sauces and soups, and the needle-like*

Aloysia triphylla, **LEMON VERBENA**

blooms of the puffball-shaped flowers are both beautiful to look at and delicious to eat when scattered over a green salad. Other Alliums *that deserve a place in the herb garden are Chinese chives,* Allium tuberosum; *the everlasting Welsh onion,* Allium fistulosum; *and the architectural Egyptian tree onion,* Allium cepa, 'Proliferum'.

Aloysia triphylla
Verbenaceae
LEMON VERBENA

CULTIVATION A half-hardy perennial, it has aromatic, narrow, lance-shaped leaves and spikes of small pale-pink flowers from midsummer. It grows to a height of 45cm–1m (18–36in) and prefers light, poor soil and full sun in a sheltered position. Propagate it by sowing seeds or taking stem cuttings in spring, planting them 60cm (2ft) apart. Harvest the leaves whenever available and the flowers in full bloom in midsummer. Grow lemon verbena as a border, container or conservatory herb.

USES Culinary, cosmetic, household
Use fresh leaves to make a delightful tisane, scent sugar, oil or vinegar or to float on the surface of a jug of chilled rum punch. Dried, the leaves can be used in pot-pourri mixtures. The essential oil from lemon verbena is prized by the perfume industry and aromatherapists.

Armoracia rusticana, **HORSERADISH**

Armoracia rusticana
Cruciferae
HORSERADISH

CULTIVATION The horseradish is a hardy perennial with long, elliptical, dark-green leaves and small, star-shaped white flowers

in midsummer. It grows to a height of 45–60cm (18–24in) and the roots generally grow from 15 to 30cm (6 to 12in) long. The horseradish prefers fertile, moist soil and light shade and to be planted 30cm (1ft) from its neighbour. Propagate it by sowing seeds or dividing the plant or taking cuttings in spring. Harvest the small, tender leaves in spring, and the roots all year round, whenever the ground is workable. Dig up the whole root and remove the top growth and peel before using. In cold areas with severe winters, store freshly-dug roots in a box of damp sand until needed. Grow it as a garden or border herb and, because horseradish can be invasive, try growing it in vertical drainage pipes, sunk into the ground.

USES Culinary, cosmetic, medicinal
Young, tender leaves taste like the root and can be added to a salad. Horseradish sauce is a mixture of grated root, lemon juice and cream.

Anethum graveolens
Umbelliferae
DILL

CULTIVATION A hardy annual, dill has aromatic, feathery, dull-green leaves with clusters of sulphur-yellow flowers from midsummer. Reaching 45cm–1m (18–36in), it prefers fertile, well-drained soil and full sun in a sheltered position. Propagate it by sowing seeds in spring and again in midsummer, thinning the seedlings to 15cm (6in) apart. Harvest the leaves and flowers whenever they are available.

Grow dill as a garden, border, container and conservatory herb.

USES Culinary, cosmetic, household, medicinal
Both the leaves and flowers have a valuable culinary role as a flavouring for fish, egg and potato dishes. The flower heads are an essential seasoning in the vinegar for dill pickles or gherkin cucumbers. Dill vinegar, dill butter and dill cream are all tasty served with dishes of summer vegetables. A tisane of dill leaves or seed is an effective digestive.

Angelica archangelica
Umbelliferae
ANGELICA

CULTIVATION A biennial, hardy herbaceous herb, it has aromatic, bright green, divided, glossy leaves with mop-headed sulphur-yellow flowers from midsummer. It reaches 1–2m (3–6ft) and prefers rich, damp soil and light shade. Propagate it by sowing seeds in late summer and early autumn, when the freshly harvested seed germinates more

Anethum graveolens, **DILL**

Angelica archangelica, **ANGELICA**

Anthriscus cerefolium, **CHERVIL**

successfully, and transplant seedlings to 75cm (2ft) apart. Harvest the young stems from late spring, the leaves at any time and the flowers from midsummer. To extend the life of the plant to three to four years, remove the flower stems and leave one flower head to provide seed. Angelica is a versatile garden, border and specimen herb.

USES Culinary, cosmetic, household, medicinal

This tall, attractive herb is grown principally for its fleshy, hollow stems that, crystallized, make the delicious green sweetmeat that cannot be equalled as a flavouring for cakes and desserts. The aromatic leaves with their distinctive flavour are also valuable in the kitchen. When used in the cooking of sharp-tasting fruits you do not need to use so much sugar.

Anthriscus cerefolium
Umbelliferae
CHERVIL

CULTIVATION Chervil is a hardy annual with aromatic, lacy, light-green leaves and delicate white clusters of flowers from late spring. It grows to a height of 20–30cm (8–12in) and prefers loamy, well-drained soil and light shade. Propagate it by sowing

seeds (it will often self-seed) from spring until late summer for a continuous crop of its lacy leaves, and thin or plant seedlings 15cm (6in) apart. Harvest the leaves and flowers whenever they are available. Pick the herb just before adding it to a dish and cut down the tall stems to stimulate the plant to produce more fresh, tender leaves. Chervil can be grown as a garden, border, container and conservatory herb.

USES Culinary, cosmetic
Chervil leaves have a subtle aniseed flavour. Simply divide them into sprigs, or pluches, for a delicious addition to salads of young leaves or as a garnish to dishes of vegetables, fish and poultry. Chop the leaves to give a delicate flavour to soups and sauces. The herb is one of the constituents of the French mixture fines herbes *which is widely used to flavour omelettes and egg dishes, as well as chicken and salads.*

Apium graveolens
Umbelliferae
SMALLAGE, WILD CELERY

CULTIVATION A hardy herbaceous biennial, smallage has aromatic, bright-green, fan-shaped leaves and greenish-yellow flowers from late summer in its second year of growth. Growing to 30cm–1m (1–3ft), it prefers fertile, well-drained soil and full sun. Propagate it by sowing seeds in late spring, thinning the seedlings to 30cm (1ft) apart. Harvest the leaves from spring to autumn and the flowers as and when they appear. Grow it outdoors only as a garden and border herb.

USES Culinary, medicinal
Smallage is a useful herb as you can use it to replace the flavour of celery in a wide range of stocks, soups and savoury dishes. The herb goes well with fish, cheese and poultry and the finely ground seed can be used instead of salt. Serve it with hard-boiled quails' eggs, for example, or as a salt-replacement in a low-salt diet.

Chop the leaves finely to make a good garnish for vegetable soup. A tisane of smallage has a sedative effect and a tea made of the dried seeds may be prescribed by herbalists as a treatment for rheumatism. Do not use during pregnancy.

Artemisia abrotanum
Compositae
SOUTHERNWOOD

CULTIVATION A hardy semi-evergreen perennial, southernwood has aromatic, grey-green, feathery or deeply indented, fern-like leaves. It grows to a height of 60cm–1m (2–3ft) and prefers light, well-drained soil and full sun. Grow it at a slight distance from culinary and medicinal herbs and give it a summer trim. A good companion plant in a hot, dry border where its foliage can soften the edge. It can usefully be grown in the vegetable garden and orchard, too, as the herb has insecticidal properties, in particular as a deterrent to cabbage butterflies. Propagate it by sowing seeds in spring or taking hardwood cuttings in late summer, planting them 60–90cm (2–3ft) apart. Harvest the leaves at any time of year. A lovely border and hedging herb.

USES Culinary, household
The cottage garden names for southernwood are 'Old Man' and 'Lad's Love'. This ancient and attractive herb can be used to make a tisane. The leaves can be placed in a wardrobe as a moth repellent. Also, place a sprig near you when you are driving on a long journey as the herb is reputed to allay tiredness. Do not use during pregnancy.

Artemisia dracunculus
Compositae
TARRAGON

CULTIVATION An almost hardy deciduous perennial, tarragon has mid-green, narrow, aromatic leaves and small, white, ball-shaped flowers in late summer. Reaching 30–60cm (1–2ft), it prefers fertile, well-drained soil and a sheltered site in full sun. Propagate it by dividing the plant in spring or taking cuttings in late summer. Harvest the leaves at any time. A useful and attractive garden, border, container and conservatory herb.

USES Culinary, household
For culinary purposes, only French tarragon is worth consideration. The flavour of this magnificent herb is one of the finest in gastronomy. French cooking has celebrated the herb's natural alliance with poultry and eggs for centuries. This affinity is illustrated by the dish of poulet à l'estragon, *which remains a classic of* cuisine bourgeoise *all over France. Tarragon is an essential herb in the cook's garden: use sprigs to flavour stocks and sauces, butter, white wine vinegar and olive oil and, along with chervil and parsley, as an essential component of* fines herbes. *A tisane of tarragon is recommended as both a digestive and tonic.*

Borago officinalis
Boraginaceae
BORAGE

CULTIVATION A hardy annual herb with hairy, dull-green, oval leaves, it has bright blue (and sometimes pink), star-shaped flowers with prominent black

Borago officinalis **BORAGE**

stamens from early summer. It grows to a height of 45–75cm (18–30in) and prefers light, well-drained soil and sun or light shade. Propagate it by sowing seeds in spring and autumn (the herb seeds itself easily in light soils) and thin or transplant the seedlings to 30cm (12in) apart. Harvest leaves and flowers at any time. A good garden, border, woodland and container herb.

USES Culinary, cosmetic, household, medicinal
Borage flowers strewn over vegetable and fruit salads and used as a garnish for sweet dishes not only look delightful, but are edible, too. Crystallized flowers will store for several weeks in an airtight container.

Calendula officinalis
Compositae
MARIGOLD

CULTIVATION This hardy annual has hairy, mid-green, tongue-shaped leaves and yellow, cream or orange, daisy-like flowers

Calendula officinalis **MARIGOLD**

Carum carvi, **CARAWAY**

Carum carvi
Umbelliferae
CARAWAY

CULTIVATION A biennial, it can be grown as an annual and is hardy. It has aromatic, feathery, light-green leaves with flat heads of tiny white flowers from midsummer. Reaching 25–45cm (10–18in), it likes rich, moist soil and full sun. Propagate it by sowing seeds in early spring or late summer, thinning seedlings to 15cm (6in) apart. Harvest the leaves and flowers when available, but, for drying, pick the flower heads before the seeds explode from their husks in late summer. Caraway is a good garden and border herb.

USES Culinary, cosmetic, medicinal
The feathery leaves of this herb resemble a cross between yarrow and chervil and their flavour is a more delicate version of the caraway seed. Add sprigs of leaves to a salad of young leaves and misticanza, or chop them finely to make a tasty addition to vegetable soups or herb butters for

beef and game. Caraway seeds are used widely in the cooking of northern and eastern Europe, especially Scandinavia and Hungary. The thick roots can be cooked.

Chamaemelum nobile
Compositae
CHAMOMILE

CULTIVATION Chamomile is a hardy evergreen perennial with aromatic, feathery, light-green leaves and white, daisy-like flowers from midsummer. Reaching a height of 20–30cm (8–12in), it prefers light, well-drained soil. Propagate it by sowing seeds in spring, taking cuttings during summer or dividing the plant in autumn, planting them 15–30cm (6–12in) apart. Harvest the leaves at any

Chamaemelum nobile, **CHAMOMILE**

from late spring. Reaching a height of 30–50cm (12–20in), it prefers moist, medium-rich soil and full sun. Propagate it by sowing seeds in spring or autumn, thinning to 15cm (6in) apart. Harvest the leaves and flowers at any time, but pick flowers you want to dry from midsummer. A garden, border, container or conservatory herb.

USES Culinary, cosmetic, household, medicinal
The shape of all daisy-type flowers reminds us of the sun, though none

more clearly than the cheerful orange-yellow marigold with its radiant petals and its golden eye. The golden marigold petals look charming strewn over a green salad and the young leaves lend a welcome peppery flavour to a plain lettuce salad. The dried flowers or petals look lovely in pot-pourri for they add a welcome note of colour; and their essential oil is used either alone or added to creams as a very effective skin treatment and in aromatherapy. As well as brightening a room like few other flowers can, a vase of fresh marigolds deters flies due to certain insecticidal properties.

time and the flowers from midsummer. Grow it as a garden, edging and carpeting herb. The non-flowering variety makes a fine chamomile lawn.

Recommended varieties Apple-scented chamomile, *C.n.* 'Flore Pleno'; non-flowering chamomile, *C.n.* 'Treneague'.

USES Culinary, cosmetic, household, medicinal
The flowers, used fresh or dried, of the apple-scented variety and German chamomile are recommended for making chamomile tea, which has a relaxing effect. You can also dry chamomile leaves and use them in pot-pourri.

Claytonia perfoliata
Portulacaceae
CLAYTONIA, WINTER PURSLANE, MINER'S LETTUCE

CULTIVATION A hardy annual with fresh, green, heart-shaped leaves and tiny white flowers borne on thin stalks above the leaf from late spring. It grows to a height of 15cm (6in) and prefers moist, fertile soil and light shade. Sow seeds in early spring and under glass in early autumn, thinning the seedlings to 10cm (4in) apart. Harvest whenever it is in leaf. A useful garden, border, edging, container and conservatory herb.

USES Culinary
Claytonia is an excellent salad herb with its bright green, generous leaves and high vitamin C and iron content. It can be a useful ingredient in the medley of salad leaves known as misticanza (page 99). The leaves are cooked like spinach.

Coriandrum sativum
Umbelliferae
CORIANDER

CULTIVATION This half-hardy annual has aromatic, toothed, bright green lower leaves and feathery upper leaves with clusters of small, pinkish-white flowers from early summer. Reaching a height of 30–45cm (12–18in), it prefers light, fertile soil and full sun. Sow seeds in early spring or under glass during autumn and thin the seedlings to 15cm (6in) apart. Water well, especially during dry weather, to promote production of the lower leaves. Harvest the leaves and flowers whenever they are available, trimming off the top growth to promote new, flavoursome leaves, or, if you primarily want the seeds, let the plant flower and cut off the seed heads when they are just turning brown in late summer. Grow it as a garden, border, container and conservatory herb.

Coriandrum sativum, **CORIANDER**

USES Culinary, horticultural, household, medicinal
Coriander is grown for both its fresh leaves and the dried seed. The fan-shaped leaves have a distinctive and unusual flavour and the aromatic seeds taste of dried orange peel. The fleshier young leaves are very good added whole to salads and vegetable dishes and are an essential ingredient in much Indian and Thai cuisine. Crushed and ground coriander seed is used to flavour cakes and biscuits and lightly spiced savoury dishes.

Eruca vesicaria sativa
Cruciferae
ROCKET

CULTIVATION Rocket is a half-hardy annual with mid-green, tongue-shaped leaves and creamy-white, four-petalled flowers. It grows up to 60cm (2ft) tall and prefers moist, fertile soil and sun or light shade. Sow seeds every few weeks from early spring, thinning seedlings to 15cm (6in) apart. Harvest the leaves at any time and the flowers from midsummer. A garden, border, container and conservatory herb.

USES Culinary
Both the leaves and flowers are excellent in green salads and the herb is one of the constituents of the Provençal winter salad known as 'mesclun'. Rocket leaves can also be cooked like spinach.

Foeniculum vulgare
Umbelliferae
FENNEL

CULTIVATION A hardy herbaceous perennial, fennel has

aromatic, feathery, mid-green or copper-bronze leaves and flat heads of sulphur yellow flowers from midsummer. It grows to a height of 1.5–2m (5–6½ft) and prefers well-drained, poor to medium-rich soil and full sun. Propagate it by sowing seeds in spring or summer or by dividing the plant in autumn, planting them 45cm (18in) apart. Harvest the leaves at any time, the flowers from midsummer and the seeds from late summer. A garden and border herb.

USES Culinary, cosmetic, medicinal
Fennel is an indispensable herb in the kitchen as its aniseed flavour has a natural affinity with fish and summer vegetables. Small sprigs of tender fennel leaves are best strewn over a green salad just before serving. Fennel seed makes a good addition to home-made bread and drained cheeses. Both the leaves and the seed can also be used to make a digestive tea that helps prevent flatulence, and seeds can be chewed to stave off hunger and relieve indigestion.

Foeniculum vulgare, **FENNEL**

Fragaria vesca
Rosaceae
WILD STRAWBERRY

CULTIVATION The wild strawberry is a hardy, evergreen perennial with mid-green, toothed, three-lobed leaves and small, white and yellow-centred flowers from early spring, producing sweet-tasting, scented, red fruits from early summer. Reaching a height of 15cm (6in), it prefers well-drained, peaty soil and a sheltered position in light shade. Propagate it by sowing seeds or dividing the plant in spring or late summer, planting them 30cm (1ft) apart. A gorgeous garden, border, edging, container and conservatory herb.

USES Culinary, cosmetic, household, medicinal
A small number of wild strawberries, freshly picked, are so perfect they need no adornment, but if you must, then add no more than a sprinkling of rose-scented sugar and a little pouring cream. Both the flowers and leaves may be added to a green salad or used as a garnish and a tisane made from the leaves is prescribed as a remedy for diarrhoea; the fruit is a laxative. The dried leaves make a delightful addition to pot-pourris.

Galium odoratum
Rubiaceae
SWEET WOODRUFF

CULTIVATION A hardy perennial, sweet woodruff has shiny, light green leaves, growing in a 'ruff' at intervals along the stems, and clusters of pure white flowers from late spring. Reaching 30cm (12in), it prefers moist, fertile

loam and light shade. Propagate it by sowing seeds in late summer or by dividing the plant during the autumn. Harvest the leaves and flowers from late spring. Grow it as a garden, border and woodland herb.

USES Culinary, household
Sweet woodruff is a delightful plant. Dried leaves of woodruff contain coumarin and this gives the herb a scent reminiscent of new-mown hay, making the dried leaves perfect for deliciously scented pillows and sachets.

Helichrysum italicum
Compositae
CURRY PLANT

CULTIVATION The curry plant is a half-hardy evergreen. It has aromatic, needle-like, silver-grey leaves and clusters of small, round, yellow flowers from midsummer. Reaching 45cm (18in), it prefers well-drained soil and full sun. Propagate it from cuttings taken in early spring or late summer, planting them 45cm (18in) apart. Harvest the leaves at any time and the flowers from midsummer while they are still bright yellow. A rewarding garden, border, container and edging herb.

USES Culinary, decorative, horticultural, household
On a warm, still day, the spicy scented foliage of the curry plant perfumes the air around it in the herb garden. The leaves can be added to soups and stews to give a delicate flavour of curry and, when separated into their individual blooms, the small yellow flowers make a pretty garnish to Indian dishes.

Hyssopus officinalis, **HYSSOP**

Hyssopus officinalis
Labiatae
HYSSOP

CULTIVATION This hardy evergreen perennial has aromatic, narrow, dark-green leaves and blue, pink or white flowers from midsummer. It grows to a height of 30–60cm (1–2ft) and prefers light, well-drained soil and full sun. Propagate it by sowing seeds or dividing the plant into sprigs or taking stem cuttings in spring and autumn. Hyssop planted in a kitchen garden lures cabbage-white butterflies from brassicas and other leaf crops. Harvest the leaves all year round and the flowers during summer and early autumn. Grow this lovely herb in the garden, border or container or as an edging.

USES Culinary, cosmetic, medicinal
The highly aromatic leaves of hyssop have a spicy taste that hints at mint and thyme. In Gascony, cooks add a sprig of hyssop to rich meat dishes and tomato preserves.

Juniperus communis, **JUNIPER**

Juniperus communis
Cupressaceae
JUNIPER

CULTIVATION Juniper is a hardy, evergreen shrub with grey-green, needle-like leaves and small, creamy-yellow flowers that appear from midsummer. Growing to a height of 1–3m (3–9ft), it prefers poor, well-drained, alkaline soil and full sun.

Propagate it by sowing seeds or taking cuttings in spring. Harvest the aromatic, navy-blue berries in their third summer when they are ripe and covered in a grey bloom. Use some berries freshly picked and dry the rest in a warm room for one to two weeks, then store them in a screw-top jar. The juniper is lovely as a garden, border, hedge or container herb. There are

dwarf, prostrate, creeping and columnar varieties available, so choose one appropriate to the site. *Plant both a male and a female, so berries will appear on the female plants.*

USES Culinary, household
Juniper berries have a distinctive and unique flavour which they impart to gin. The berries can also be used to season game and rich meats beautifully and, added to a wine marinade, give a delicious flavour to slowly cooked meat dishes. Pâtés and terrines made from pork or goose are improved by the addition of a few crushed juniper berries. Do not eat juniper during pregnancy.

Laurus nobilis
Lauraceae
BAY, SWEET BAY, LAUREL

CULTIVATION A semi-hardy evergreen tree with aromatic, glossy, mid-green, lance-shaped leaves and small, creamy-white flowers from midsummer. It reaches a height of up to 8m (26ft) and prefers a sheltered position, rich, well-drained soil and sun or light shade. Propagate it by taking 10cm (4in) stem cuttings in late summer. Plant them in sandy soil in a frost-free corner of the garden or under glass. Harvest the leaves at any time when using them straight away, but, for drying, pick them from midsummer. Bay is an elegant garden, border, hedging, specimen, container and conservatory herb.
Recommended varieties
Common green bay, *L.n.*; golden bay, *L.n.* 'Aurea'; willow leaf bay, *L.n. angustifolia.*

USES Culinary, cosmetic, household, medicinal
Bay leaves are immensely valuable in the kitchen. When young they are mid-green, then they gradually thicken and darken with age until they resemble glossy leather, the fragrance of the fresh leaf being balsamic, a delicate balance of lemon and nutmeg, becoming spicier and less subtle as it dries. Apart from the bay leaf's outstanding culinary uses, the herb is a most handsome plant of Mediterranean origin and can live for over 50 years. For a fine specimen tree, one should trim the leaves to shape in late spring.

Lavandula angustifolia
Labiatae
LAVENDER

CULTIVATION A hardy evergreen shrub, lavender has aromatic, slim, grey-green leaves and mauve, blue, white or pink flowers. It grows to a height of 30–75cm (12–30in) and prefers poor, well-drained soil and full sun. Propagate it by taking stem cuttings in spring or summer or by dividing the plant in the autumn, planting them 30cm (1ft) apart. Harvest the flowers as they open and the leaves all year round. Lavender is a versatile garden, border, hedge and container herb.
Recommended varieties Blue-flowered, *L.a.* 'Munstead'; white-flowered, *L.a.* 'Nana Alba'; purple-flowered, *L.a.* 'Hidcote'; French lavender, *L. stoechas*; silver-leaved purple-blue, *L.* 'Sawyer's'; Dutch lavender, *L.* x *intermedia* 'Vera'.

USES Culinary, cosmetic, household, medicinal

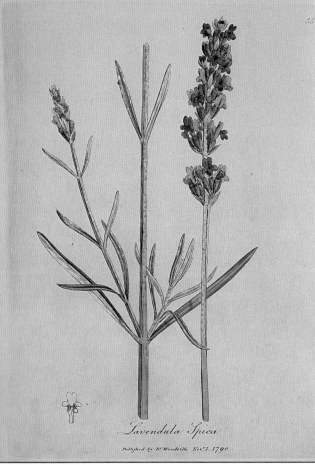

Lavandula angustifolia, **LAVENDER**

This Mediterranean herb is an essential one in both the house and the garden for its delightful fragrance and charming appearance. In the kitchen, both the leaves and the flowers can be used to flavour sweet dishes and creams and, medicinally, a tisane of lavender is a calming antidote to anxiety and depression. The oil of lavender is widely used in cosmetics as it is a good skin cleanser.

The dried flowers of lavender are an important component of many pot-pourri mixtures and herbal wreaths and their scent will discourage moths and insects.

Levisticum officinalis
Umbelliferae
LOVAGE

CULTIVATION Lovage is a hardy herbaceous perennial with aromatic, toothed, glossy, dark-green leaves and lime-green umbels of flowers from late summer. It reaches 60cm–2m (2–6ft) and prefers moist, fertile soil and full sun or light shade. Propagate it by sowing seeds in spring or summer or by dividing the plant in spring or autumn, planting them 60cm (2ft) apart.

Levisticum officinalis, **LOVAGE**

Harvest the leaves at any time and the seed in late summer. Perfect both as a garden and a border herb.

USES Culinary, medicinal
The flavour of lovage leaves is reminiscent of celery and angelica and the herb has the unusual characteristic of giving a yeasty, almost meat-like flavour to other ingredients that can make vegetarian dishes more appealing to meat eaters. The seed is excellent added to wholemeal bread dough and a lovage leaf butter is an appetizing garnish for vegetable soups, potatoes, beetroot and other root vegetables. Lovage tea is known for its diuretic properties. Lovage should not be used during pregnancy.

Malva moschata
Malvaceae
MUSK MALLOW

CULTIVATION The musk mallow is a semi-evergreen perennial with slightly aromatic, feathery, bright green leaves and white or rose-coloured flowers from midsummer. Reaching 60cm–1m

(2–3ft), it prefers well-drained, poor soil and full sun. Propagate it by sowing seeds or taking stem cuttings in the spring, planting them 60cm (2ft) apart. Harvest the leaves and flowers at any time. A very pretty garden and border herb.

USES Culinary, cosmetic
The petals of the edible flowers of musk mallow can be used to decorate summer desserts and sorbets, while whole flowers look pretty embedded in ice plates and bowls. The Malvaceae *family has over 1,000 members and they are valued for the gum-like substance made by crushing the seeds that is a remedy for inflammation.*

Melissa officinalis
Labiatae
LEMON BALM

CULTIVATION Lemon balm is a hardy herbaceous perennial with aromatic, oval, puckered, dull-green or variegated leaves and tiny white flowers from midsummer. It grows to 60cm–1m (2–3ft) and prefers poor, moist soil and full sun or light shade. Propagate it by sowing seeds or taking stem cuttings in spring, or dividing the plant in the autumn, planting them 50cm (20in) apart. Harvest the leaves from spring to autumn and the flowers during the summer. Lemon balm can be grown as a garden or border herb.

USES Culinary, cosmetic, household, medicinal
The leaves of this vigorous and easy-to-grow herb make a refreshing tisane known as Melissa tea. The tea can be served hot with honey or cold with ice cubes. Alternatively, a sprig of lemon balm may also be added to a pot of *Earl Grey or Ceylon tea. Use it, too, to give custards and ice-cream a delicate lemon flavour by steeping the herb in hot cream or milk, then using the flavoured liquid in the recipe. Small, tender leaves are delicious added to a green salad, or, chopped, in chilled summer soups and hot* vegetable dishes. Lemon balm vinegar *is easily made by slipping two or three sprigs of the herb into a bottle of white wine vinegar and leaving the bottle in a sunny place for two weeks before using. Medicinally, a handful of fresh leaves held against the skin are a soothing treatment for insect bites and sores.*

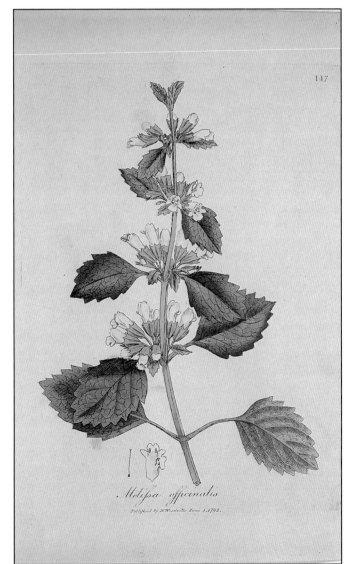

Melissa officinalis, **LEMON BALM**

Mentha species
Labiatae
MINT

CULTIVATION A hardy herbaceous perennial, mint has highly aromatic, oval or spear-shaped leaves and white, pink or pale mauve flowers. It grows to a height of 1cm–1m ($\frac{1}{2}$in–3ft) and prefers rich, damp soil and sun or light shade. Because the plant spreads easily, sending out runners underground, plant mint in a bed on its own or in a container sunk into the ground. Plant mint 30cm (1ft) apart. Harvest the leaves from early spring until the first frost and the flowers from midsummer. An attractive and useful garden, border and container herb.
Recommended varieties Apple mint, *M. suaveolens*, or Bowles mint, *M. x villosa alopecuroides*; Corsican mint, *M. requienii*; eau-de-cologne mint and lemon mint, *M. x piperita citrata*; ginger mint, *M. x gentilis*; Japanese mint, *M.*

Mentha, **MINT**

arvensis; pennyroyal, *M. pulegium*; spearmint and Moroccan mint, *M. spicata*; peppermint, *M. x piperita*; water mint, *M. aquatica*.

USES Culinary, cosmetic, household, medicinal
Defining and classifying all 2,000 members of the 'Labiatae' family – whose 40 species of mint form just one branch – is a formidable task, and an ever-growing one, since the mint hybridizes easily. However, the most common culinary mints number just a dozen or so.

The distinctive essential oil in the plant is menthol and its refreshing flavour has made mint popular in cuisines all over the world – from the cooling yoghurt drink from India known as 'lassi' to the well-known mint sauce that British cooks serve with roast lamb. Both fresh and dried mint are especially popular in Mediterranean cooking. A tisane made from the leaves, served hot or chilled, is delightful and candied mint leaves make a charming decoration for summer desserts and chilled drinks. See the recipe for Southern Mint Julep on page 162.

Monarda didyma
Labiatae
BERGAMOT, BEE BALM

CULTIVATION A perennial, hardy, herbaceous herb with aromatic, oval, pointed, mid-green leaves and shaggy heads of tubular scarlet flowers in late summer. Reaching a height of 50cm–1m (18–36in), it prefers fertile, well-drained soil and full sun or light shade. Propagate it by taking root cuttings in spring or autumn, or stem cuttings in summer, planting them 45cm (18in) apart. Harvest the leaves

Monarda didyma, **BERGAMOT**

and flowers at any time, but pick flowers you want to dry from late summer. Grow it as a border herb and in fruit and vegetable gardens as it attracts bees.
Recommended varieties
Purple-flowered bergamot, *M.* 'Blue Stocking'; pink-flowered bergamot, *M.* 'Croftway Pink'.

USES Culinary, cosmetic, household, medicinal
Both the leaves and flowers of the scarlet-flowered bergamot are valuable in the kitchen. The flavour of the aromatic leaf is a blend of mint and lemon. The flowers – fresh or dried – give a distinctive flavour to green or blackleaf teas. Indeed, the tisane made from the fresh or dried leaves is known as Oswego Tea after the North American Indians who drank it. The separated tubular blooms look and taste delightful when strewn over a green or fruit salad. The flowers are lovely in pot-pourri mixtures.

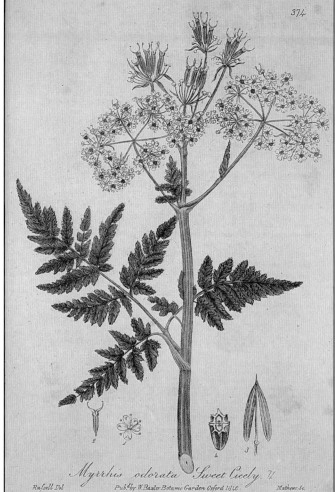

Myrrhis odorata, **SWEET CICELY**

Myrrhis odorata
Umbelliferae
SWEET CICELY

CULTIVATION Sweet cicely is a hardy herbaceous perennial with light to mid-green, aromatic, lacy leaves and flat umbels of white flowers from late spring, with attractive, slim, curved seeds following. It prefers fertile soil and light shade and grows to a height of 1m (3ft). Propagate it by sowing seeds in autumn or by dividing the plant in late spring, planting them 60cm (2ft) apart. Harvest the leaves at any time, the flowers from late spring and the seeds from midsummer. Grow it in a garden or border; especially good for orchards or bee gardens as it flowers early.

USES Culinary, household
This herb's botanical name comes from the Greek word for perfume,

and, to my mind, no herb garden seems complete without this lovely herb that springs into leaf very early in the year. The leaves, flowers and seeds all have a delicate aniseed flavour and each play valuable roles in the kitchen. The small young leaves are excellent added to a green salad or misticanza, the flowers are an attractive addition to fruit compôte or summer tart and the seeds give a delightful flavour to fruit syrup or apple pie. Like angelica, the leaves of sweet cicely can be used to 'sweeten' sharp-tasting fruit like rhubarb, gooseberries, and blackcurrants, so less sugar need be used.

Myrtus communis
Myrtaceae
MYRTLE

CULTIVATION A half-hardy evergreen perennial, the myrtle has small, shiny, lance-shaped leaves and creamy-white flowers from midsummer. Reaching 2–3m (6–10ft), it prefers a sheltered site with moderately rich, well-drained soil and full sun. Plant 1m (3ft) apart. Harvest the leaves all year round, the scented flowers when in bloom, the blue-black berries in early autumn and dry the leaves and flowers from midsummer. A handsome garden, hedge, conservatory and container herb.
Recommended variety *M.c. tarentina.*

USES Culinary, cosmetic, household
The plant is native to southern Europe and sprigs are used to flavour pork and lamb in Tuscan and Cretan cooking. The fresh berries are added to some Mediterranean dishes and the dried berries used as a seasoning for

meat in Turkey. Short branches of myrtle placed over hot charcoal just before barbecuing meat or fish give a delicious juniper-like flavour to the food. Myrtle flowers are edible, too. Both the flowers and the leaves are lovely dried in pot-pourri.

Nepeta cataria
Labiatae
CATMINT, CATNIP

CULTIVATION Catmint is a perennial, hardy herbaceous herb. It has aromatic, downy, grey-green leaves with spikes of small, soft blue or white flowers from early summer. It grows to a height of 45cm–1m (18–36in) and prefers well-drained, poorish soil and sun. Propagate it by taking softwood cuttings in spring or by dividing the plant in late summer, planting the young plant pieces 30cm (12in) apart. Harvest the leaves and flowers whenever they are available, picking leaves you intend drying from midsummer.

Nepeta cataria, **CATMINT**

A lovely garden, border, edging and container herb, it deters insects and beetles so grow it as a companion plant in kitchen, fruit and herb gardens. For edging, the low-growing catmint, *N. mussinii* is recommended.

USES Culinary, cosmetic, household, medicinal
Both the toothed, triangular leaves and the scented blue flowers are highly aromatic. The fresh leaves, which are rich in vitamin C, make a fresh, healthy tisane, and can be used to flavour meat pâtés and terrines. The young shoots may be added to a green salad. Catmint contains several volatile oils that have medicinal and horticultural value.

Ocimum basilicum
Labiatae
BASIL

CULTIVATION Basil is a tender annual, bearing aromatic, oval, pointed, light-green leaves and clusters of small white flowers from late summer. It grows to a height of 20–45cm (8–18in) and prefers rich, damp soil and full sun in a sheltered position or under glass. Propagate it by sowing seeds in spring, thinning or transplanting the seedlings to 20cm (8in) apart. Harvest the leaves and flowers at any time, removing the flowers as they appear so the plants grow more leaves. It is a lovely garden, border, edging, container and conservatory herb.
Recommended varieties Greek basil, *O.b. minimum*; French basil, *O.b. communis*; Opal basil, *O.b. purpurascens*; Lemon basil, *O.b. citriodorum*; Genoese basil *O.b.* 'Genovese'; Aniseed basil.

USES Culinary, cosmetic, household, medicinal
No herb evokes so strongly the cooking of Italy and the South of France as the clove-like fragrance of basil. The leaves are fragile and highly aromatic, so add them whole to salads and vegetable dishes, but chopped or pounded to sauces, especially those based on olive oil such as pesto. The small-leaved Greek basil is the best for sauces, while the fleshy-leaved Italian basil is recommended for salads and pesto. The purple-leaved Opal basil is beautiful for garnishes and for adding to salads, but has a less pronounced flavour than the other varieties.

Origanum species
Labiatae
MARJORAM

CULTIVATION Marjoram is a hardy herbaceous perennial with aromatic, woolly, small, oval leaves and white or pink flowers from midsummer. Reaching 15–30cm (6–12in), it prefers poor soil and full sun. Propagate

Origanum majorana,
SWEET MARJORAM

marjoram by sowing seeds in spring or by dividing the plant in spring or autumn or by taking stem cuttings during the summer, planting them 30cm (1ft) apart. Harvest the leaves and flowers at any time to use fresh, but dry the leaves in midsummer just as the plant comes into flower. A useful garden, edging, container and conservatory herb.

Recommended varieties Sweet, or knotted, marjoram, *O. majorana*; pot or French marjoram, *O. onites*, also the rarely flowering *O. onites* 'crinkle-leaved types'; Oregano, *O. vulgare*; golden marjoram, *O. vulgare aureum*; winter marjoram, *O. vulgare hirtum*.

USES Culinary, cosmetic, medicinal
The herb is used for tisanes, and in tomato, egg, fish and cheese dishes. Marjoram leaves contain thymol, which is a powerful antiseptic and the delicious flavour of the herb is akin to thyme but spicier. Marjoram is one of the characteristic herbs of the eastern Mediterranean and, on the hillsides of Italy and Greece, wild marjoram, which is known as oregano, flowers freely, forming sheets of pale pink.

Pelargonium species
Geraniaceae
GERANIUM

CULTIVATION A tender evergreen perennial with highly-scented, green or variegated decorative leaves, usually toothed or deeply cut, and white or pale pink flowers from midsummer. It grows to a height of 30cm–1m (1–3ft) and prefers

gritty potting compost in full sun or light shade. Propagate it by sowing seeds or taking tip cuttings in spring or late summer. Harvest the leaves and edible flowers all year round. An excellent garden, border, container or window-box herb that can be also be grown indoors quite easily.

Recommended varieties Rose-scented, *P. graveolens*; rose-peppermint, *P. tomentosum*; rose-lemon, *P. radens*; pineapple, *P. x fragrans*; orange, *P.* 'Prince of Orange'.

USES Culinary, cosmetic, household, medicinal
The geranium's highly aromatic leaves easily transfer their flavour to sugar, custards, cakes and other sweet dishes and both the leaves and flowers make an attractive and edible garnish to summer desserts and delightful tisanes. The dried leaves can be added to pot-pourris and the essential oils in the herb are used in the perfume industry and aromatherapy.

Petroselinum crispum
Umbelliferae
PARSLEY

CULTIVATION A hardy biennial with aromatic, bright green leaves that are either curly or flat and trifoliate with flat heads of yellow-green flowers. Reaching 25–45cm (10–18in), it prefers moist, fertile soil in sun or light shade. Sow seeds outdoors in late spring or, under glass, at any time of year, remembering not to cover the seeds with soil and to thin the plants to 15cm (6in) apart. Harvest the leaves at any time, the flowers from midsummer. An attractive and

useful garden, border, edging, container and conservatory herb.
Recommended varieties Curled parsley; turnip-rooted Hamburg parsley, *P.c.* 'Tuberosum'; Flat-leaf Italian or French parsley, *P.c.* 'Neapolitan'.

USES Culinary, cosmetic, household, medicinal
Every part of the parsley plant is useful in the kitchen – the leaves, stalks and roots all have a part to play in cooking, and have done since the time of Pliny. The delicious flavour gives a well-rounded taste to soups and sauces and works wonderfully well with all fish and vegetable dishes. The leaves of flat-leaf parsley also make a simple and appealing garnish. A French persillade *is composed of finely chopped parsley and garlic; an Italian* gremolata *is finely chopped parsley combined with grated zest of lemon, used as the final garnish to meat dishes like* osso buco. *Parsley is also the essential herb in a classic* maître d'hôtel *butter, which is the ideal finishing touch to a dish such as grilled steak or fish.*

Petroselinum crispum, **PARSLEY**

Pimpinella anisum
Umbelliferae
ANISE, ANISEED

CULTIVATION Aniseed is a half-hardy annual with aromatic, toothed, bright-green lower leaves, lacy upper leaves and clusters of small white blooms from midsummer. Reaching a height of 40cm (15in), it prefers rich, well-drained soil and full sun. Sow seeds in mid-spring, thinning the seedlings to 12cm (4in) apart. Harvest the leaves and flowers whenever they are available and the seed from late summer. Grow it as a garden, border, container and conservatory herb.

USES Culinary, cosmetic, household, medicinal
The aromatic leaves have a more subtle flavour than the seeds, indeed whole leaves make an excellent addition to a green salad. Green, freshly-gathered seeds are often more popular than the dried seed. Aniseed is chiefly used in the cooking of the Middle East and India and in some European breads and biscuits. The seeds are used in aperitifs like pastis and anisette.

Portulaca oleracea
Portulacaceae
PURSLANE

CULTIVATION Purslane is a half-hardy annual with fleshy, tongue-shaped, light green leaves and small, daisy-like yellow flowers. It grows to a height of 15cm (6in) and prefers moist, fertile soil and sun. Sow seeds outdoors in late spring or under glass at any time of year, thinning the seedlings to 15cm (6in) apart.

Pimpinella anisum, **ANISE**

Portulaca oleracea, **PURSLANE**

Harvest the leaves at any time, the flowers from midsummer. A useful garden, border, container and conservatory herb.

Recommended varieties
Common, or green, purslane, Yellow-leaved purslane, *P. sativa.*

USES Culinary
For centuries, this herb has been widely grown in southern Europe and the Middle East. It is a native of southern France, where the herb grows wild, and its leaves, which are rich in vitamin C, are valuable in salads, while the yellow blooms can be used to garnish a green salad. In Provence the herb is cooked, either alone or mixed with spinach, as a green vegetable. In the past, in the Midi, the reddish stalks and fleshy leaves were pickled in vinegar for winter eating.

Rosa species
Rosaceae
ROSE

CULTIVATION The rose is a hardy deciduous perennial with oval leaves on prickly stems and fragrant or unscented blooms that produce green, yellow or red hips. Reaching up to 2m (6ft), or taller for climbing species, it prefers well-drained, moderately fertile soil and sun or light shade. Propagate it by taking cuttings in late summer and plant them 1–2m (3–6ft) apart. Repeat flowering types can be dead-headed to produce further blooms. Harvest the flowers from early summer and the hips from late summer until the first frosts. A beautiful garden, border, hedging, container and conservatory herb.

Recommended varieties Pink and red, scented varieties, like 'Madame Isaac Pereire', 'Guinee', 'Alec's Red', and Damask roses.

USES Culinary, cosmetic, household, medicinal
Use rose petals to make preserves and scented vinegar and sugar. Rose-hips can be used to make syrups and jams.

Rosmarinus officinalis
Labiatae
ROSEMARY

CULTIVATION Rosemary is a hardy evergreen with aromatic, needle-shaped, grey-green leaves and scented, blue, white, pink or mauve flowers that appear from early spring and at any time during mild weather. Reaching 30cm–2m (1–6ft), it prefers slightly limy, well-drained soil and a sheltered position in full sun. Propagate it by sowing seeds in spring or by taking tip cuttings during summer and early autumn. Plant them 45cm–1m (18–36in) apart. Harvest the leaves and flowers at any time. An attractive and extremely versatile garden, border, hedging and container herb.

Recommended varieties Lilac-blue-flowered wild rosemary; blue-flowered R.o. 'Suffolk Blue'; pink-flowered R.o. 'Majorcan Pink'; white-flowered R.o. albus; pale blue-flowered R.o. 'Miss Jessopp's Upright'; blue-flowered prostrate R.o. prostratus; semi-prostrate half-hardy blue-flowered R.o. 'Severn Sea'.

USES Culinary, household, medicinal
Rosemary grows wild around the shores of the Mediterranean and is used to give a distinctive flavour to the cooking of Provence and Southern Italy. Sprigs of rosemary added to pork, lamb and fish dishes bring out their flavour and a faggot of rosemary branches burnt over charcoal when barbecuing smells and tastes good. The highly aromatic leaves give a delightful flavour to honey, sugar and syrups. A tisane of rosemary tea is an effective digestive and the essential oil from the herb is antiseptic.

Rosmarinus officinalis, **ROSEMARY**

Rumex acetosa
Polygonaceae
SORREL

CULTIVATION Sorrel is a hardy perennial with bright green, spear-shaped leaves and rust-coloured, small, disc-shaped flowers from midsummer. Reaching 30–90cm (1–3ft), it prefers fertile, moist soil and light shade. Propagate it by sowing seeds in spring or by dividing the plant during the autumn. Thin seedlings to 25cm (10in) apart. Harvest the leaves whenever they are available. A useful garden, border, edging and container herb.
Recommended varieties *R.a.* 'Large de Belleville' and 'Oseille de Belleville'.

USES Culinary, household, medicinal
The delicious, lemony flavour of young sorrel leaves is one of the luxuries of springtime. This citrus-like sharpness makes sorrel an admirable partner to rich food or oily fish such as salmon, mackerel or trout. Sorrel sauce also goes well with eggs and rich meats.

The herb is also cooked with spinach to develop the flavour of the vegetable. It is rich in vitamins A, B1 and C.

Ruta graveolens
Rutaceae
RUE

CULTIVATION A hardy, evergreen perennial, rue has small, aromatic, blue-green leaves and yellowy-green, daisy-like flowers from midsummer. It grows to a height of 30–60cm (1–2ft) and prefers poorish, dry soil and a sheltered site in full sun. Propagate it by sowing seeds in spring or by dividing the plant or taking stem cuttings in late summer. Harvest the leaves all year round and the flowers from midsummer. A pretty garden, border, edging and container herb.
Recommended varieties *R.g.* 'Jackman's Blue'; *R.g.* 'Variegata'.

USES Culinary, household, medicinal

Salvia horminum
Labiatae
CLARY

CULTIVATION Clary is a hardy annual with green-veined bracts, coloured in shades of pink, purple, blue and white from midsummer. It reaches 30–45cm (12–18in) and prefers moderately rich soil and full sun. Sow seeds sparingly in spring and thin the plants to 10cm (4in) apart. Harvest the leaves whenever they are available. It is a pretty garden, border, container and conservatory herb.

USES Culinary, household
The attractive bracts of clary are delightful strewn over a leaf salad and small sprigs plucked from the top of each stem make an excellent edible garnish. Leaves and sprays of clary also dry well for use in pot-pourris and dried herb wreaths.

Salvia officinalis
Labiatae
SAGE

CULTIVATION A hardy evergreen perennial, sage has aromatic, velvety leaves that are grey, green, purple or variegated according to the variety and blue, pink or mauve, scented flowers from midsummer. Reaching 30–75cm (12–30in), it prefers light, well-drained soil and full sun. Propagate it by sowing seeds in spring or by taking tip cuttings from spring

Salvia sclarea, **CLARY SAGE**

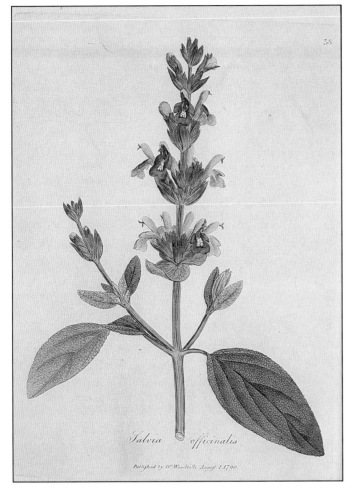

Salvia officinalis, **SAGE**

USES Culinary, cosmetic, household, medicinal
The happy marriage of sage with rich meats is well exploited by Italian cooks who use the herb widely in savoury dishes. Sage vinegar and sage butter make good accompaniments to pork and veal sausages. Sage tea is recommended as a nerve and blood tonic and as a digestive.

Sambucus nigra
Caprifoliaceae
ELDER

CULTIVATION Elder is a deciduous perennial shrub or tree with aromatic, oval, toothed, mid-green leaves and flat umbels of tiny, creamy-white flowers from early summer. It grows to a height and spread of 3–5m (10–16ft). Propagate it by sowing ripe berries or taking hardwood cuttings during spring or late summer. Prune elder to shape during the winter. Harvest the flower heads as soon as they appear from early summer onwards and the berries from late summer. Grow elder as a garden and specimen herb.

USES Culinary, cosmetic, household, medicinal
Elderflower, with its lovely muscatel flavour, can magically transform the taste of light summer desserts, sorbets and ice-creams and a syrup made with the blossom can be stored for use in winter. The shiny, purple-black berries, which are rich in vitamin C, make splendid pies and summer puddings. Elderflower can also be put to medicinal use as cool elderflower water is recommended for bathing sun-burnt skin and the eyes. A glass of elderflower champagne is a delicious non-alcoholic drink.

Sambucus nigra, **ELDER**

Sanguisorba minor
Rosaceae
SALAD BURNET

CULTIVATION Salad burnet is a hardy herbaceous perennial with leaves that are formed from pairs of mid-green, toothed leaflets and it has pinky-green, ball-shaped flowers. It grows to a height of 10–40cm (4–16in) and prefers poorish, alkaline soil and sun or light shade. Propagate it by sowing seeds in spring or autumn. Harvest the leaves at any time – doing this regularly throughout the growing season promotes the growth of new leaves – and the flowers from midsummer. A very useful garden, border and edging herb.

USES Culinary, cosmetic, medicinal
The herb grows wild in Provence and its decorative, toothed leaves have a slight taste of cucumber. Add salad burnet leaves to green salads and use as a garnish with some borage flowers for summer dishes and chilled wine cups. If a few salad burnet leaves are added to cool water, the result is a soothing lotion for sunburn.

until autumn. Harvest the leaves all year round – although they are at their best during the spring – and the flowers from early summer. Grow sage as a garden, border, container, edging and hedging herb.
Recommended varieties
Spanish narrow-leaf sage, *S. lavandulifolia*; prostrate sage, *S. prostrata*; gold variegated sage, *S.o.* 'Icterina'; broad-leafed sage, *S.o.* broad-leaved variety ; purple or red sage, *S.o.* 'Purpurascens'; green- pink- or white-leaved sage, *S.o.* 'Tricolor' with a mild flavour.
S. rutilans PINEAPPLE SAGE
A half-hardy annual with smooth, red-tipped, mid-green, pineapple-scented leaves and narrow, scarlet, trumpet-shaped flowers. Both leaves and flowers are excellent for flavouring and garnishing sweet dishes.
S. sclarea CLARY SAGE
A hardy biennial member of the sage family with large-toothed, hairy leaves and aromatic, columnar lilac and white flowers.

Santolina chamaecyparissus
Compositae
SANTOLINA

CULTIVATION Santolina, a hardy evergreen perennial, has aromatic, narrow, feathery, silver-grey leaves and bright yellow, button-shaped flowers. Reaching 23–45cm (9–18in), it prefers poor, sandy soil and full sun. Its grey foliage and neat habit make it ideal for edging, though clip it to shape during the summer. Propagate it by taking tip cuttings from spring until late summer, planting them 30cm (12in) apart. Harvest the leaves all year round and the flowers from midsummer. Grow santolina as a garden, border, edging and container herb.
Recommended varieties *S.c.* 'Lemon Queen'; *S. virens.*

USES Household, medicinal
This attractive herb is also known as cotton lavender.

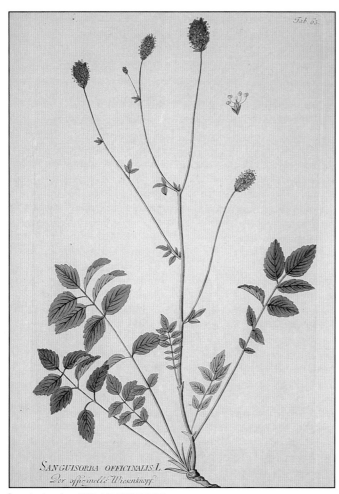

Sanguisorba minor, **SALAD BURNET**

Satureja montana
Labiatae
WINTER SAVORY

CULTIVATION Winter savory is a hardy evergreen perennial with aromatic, narrow, dull-green leaves and pale mauve flowers in late summer. Reaching 30cm (1ft), it prefers well-drained, alkaline soil and full sun. Propagate it by sowing seeds or dividing the plant in late summer, planting them 30cm (1ft) apart. Harvest the leaves at any time and the flowers when they bloom. Winter savory is an attractive and useful garden, border and edging herb.
Recommended varieties
Creeping winter savory, *S. repanda.*

USES Culinary, cosmetic, medicinal
The flavour of winter savory resembles a peppery thyme, making the herb useful in dishes of rich meats and game. A more valuable variety, however, is the annual summer savory, S. hortensis, *whose paler green leaves and pale pink flowers have a more delicate flavour. Summer savory is a famous partner for broad beans and, indeed, the herb does go well with them and grows well alongside the vegetable, too. Finely chopped leaves of either savory make an excellent flavouring for butter.*

Stachys officinalis
Labiatae
BETONY

CULTIVATION A hardy perennial herbaceous herb, it has aromatic, felty, dull green leaves with spikes of pink or purple flowers from late summer. It reaches 45–60cm (18–24in) and prefers fertile soil and light shade. Propagate it by sowing seeds in early spring or by dividing clumps in spring or autumn, planting them 30cm (1ft) apart. Harvest the leaves at any time and the flowers from late summer. It is a good garden, border and woodland herb, but it can become invasive.

USES Culinary, medicinal
Betony's aromatic oval leaves are highly valued for making medicinal teas and tisanes as the herb has sedative and antispasmodic properties, particularly valuable in the treatment of migraines and nervous exhaustion.

Symphytum officinale
Boraginaceae
COMFREY

CULTIVATION A hardy, herbaceous perennial with long, lance-shaped, dull-green leaves, comfrey has mauve-blue, bell-shaped flowers from midsummer. It grows to a height of 1m (3ft) and prefers well-drained, fertile soil. Start with a small plant and, for more plants, divide it during early spring or late summer, planting them 50cm (20in) apart. A useful garden or border herb.

USES Culinary, horticultural, household, medicinal
Comfrey is a vigorous and attractive plant with many valuable medicinal and horticultural qualities. The leaves are rich in vitamins A, C and B12 and in the minerals calcium, phosphorus and potassium. They also have a higher protein content than any other vegetable. Recent research has indicated that internal use of comfrey should be avoided until further

Symphytum officinale, **COMFREY**

Tanacetum parthenium, **FEVERFEW**

USES Culinary, cosmetic, household, medicinal
Due to the bitter flavour, the herb has limited culinary use, but both the leaves and the flowers can be used to make a mildly sedative tisane. Herbalists, however, have been making use of feverfew as a treatment for headaches for centuries. More recently, scientists have supported their assertions, establishing that feverfew taken each day is an effective treatment for migraine. Do not use during pregnancy.

Tanacetum vulgare
Compositae
TANSY

CULTIVATION The tansy is a hardy herbaceous perennial with aromatic, indented and toothed, bright green leaves and buttercup-yellow, button-shaped flowers from midsummer. It grows to a height of 1–1.25m (3–4ft) and prefers light, well-drained soil and sun or light shade. Propagate it by sowing seeds in spring or by dividing

the plant in autumn. Harvest the leaves when they are available from spring until early winter and the flowers from midsummer. A pretty garden, border and container herb.

USES Culinary, cosmetic, household, medicinal
The bitter-tasting tansy leaf should be used with discretion in cooking. The herb has given its name to the springtime dishes of fruit with custard, usually made with rhubarb or gooseberries, that date from Elizabethan cooking. Although John Evelyn recommends cooking the leaves with butter and serving them with orange juice and sugar, I regard tansy more as a decorative herb for growing in the herb garden and orchard as its insecticidal properties are very useful there. Both the leaves and flowers can be picked in midsummer for drying for pot-pourris and filling anti-moth sachets. Although a lotion made with tansy is recommended for bathing bruises, sensitive skins may react to the herb's toxicity. Do not use during pregnancy.

Teucrium chamaedrys
Labiatae
WALL GERMANDER

CULTIVATION A hardy evergreen perennial with aromatic, mid-green leaves, similar in shape to an oak leaf, and mauve-pink flowers from midsummer. It grows to a height of 10–20cm (4–8in) and prefers well-drained soil and full sun. Propagate it by sowing seeds or taking cuttings in late spring or by dividing the plant in early autumn, planting them 30cm (1ft) apart. Harvest the leaves at any time but principally during midsummer,

information about its effects is known. A benefit for gardeners is that, if steeped in water for 3–4 weeks, the leaves can be used to make an organic fertilizer, specially suited to potatoes and tomatoes. Wilted leaves make an excellent soil mulch for garden beds.

Tanacetum parthenium
Compositae
FEVERFEW

CULTIVATION Feverfew is a hardy perennial with aromatic, lacy-edged, lime or yellow-green leaves and single or double, daisy-like, white flowers from early summer. Reaching 45–60cm (18–24in), it prefers well-drained, medium soil and full sun. Propagate it by sowing seeds in spring or divide the plant in autumn and one can take stem cuttings from the plant in summer. Harvest the leaves whenever they are available and the flowers from midsummer. A lovely garden, border, container and conservatory herb.

and the flowers when they are available. An attractive garden, edging and container herb.

USES Cosmetic, household, medicinal
A tisane made from wall germander is good for gout and rheumatism.

Thymus species
Labiatae
THYME

CULTIVATION Thyme is an evergreen perennial with small, aromatic, green or yellow, lance-shaped leaves and pink, purple or white flowers. Growing to a height of 2–30cm (½–12in), it prefers well-drained, alkaline soil and full sun. Propagate it by planting seeds in spring or by layering or taking stem cuttings in summer or by dividing the plant during autumn, planting them 15–30cm (6–12in) apart. Harvest the leaves at any time and the flowers from early summer. An excellent garden, border, edging, container and conservatory herb.
Recommended varieties
Garden thyme, *T. vulgaris*; Lemon thyme, *T. x citriodorus*; Silver-leaf thyme.

USES Culinary, cosmetic, household, medicinal
Thyme is a native of the Mediterranean where the clumps of pink-flowered wild thyme growing on the rocky hillsides of Provence and Calabria scent the air and is used to give flavour to the cooking of the region. A sprig of thyme is part of the classic bouquet garni*, and British cooking, too, has made much use of the herb since the Middle Ages. The herb's ability to aid digestion*

Thymus, **THYME**

makes thyme a natural ally of rich meats like goose and game, roast beef and pork. Thyme is a herb that dries supremely well and is one of the eight herbs in the blend known as herbes de Provence. *Dried thyme is added to pot-pourris and makes one of the most beneficial of all tisanes as it stimulates the circulation and even speeds recovery from a hangover.*

Tilia cordata
Tiliaceae
LIME

CULTIVATION A deciduous tree, the lime has heart-shaped, mid-green, glossy leaves and scented, creamy-yellow flowers with yellow-green flattened false petals like bracts from midsummer. It grows up to 10m (33ft) high and prefers moist, moderately fertile soil and full sun or light shade. Propagate it by sowing seeds or taking stem cuttings in spring, planting them 10m (33ft) apart. Harvest the flowers as soon as they bloom in midsummer, dry them in a dark, airy place and store in a screw-top jar.

Tilia cordata, **LIME**

USES Culinary, cosmetic, medicinal
The fragrant lime tree deserves a place in any large garden. The mature tree has a handsome shape and, in midsummer, the scent from the clusters of flowers travels some distance. Lime flowers attract bees, and lime-flower honey is particularly sweet and delectable.

The fresh or dried flowers can be used to make a soothing tea or tisane, sometimes known as linden tea, that is often served as a digestive or a calming tonic and an infusion of lime flowers makes an excellent skin toner.

Trigonella foenum-graecum
Leguminosae
FENUGREEK

CULTIVATION A tender annual, it has small, oval, bright-green leaves appearing in threes and creamy-yellow flowers from midsummer. It grows to a height of 30–60cm (12–24in) and prefers fertile, well-drained soil. Propagate it by sowing seeds in spring and midsummer, thinning the seedlings to 15cm (6in) apart. Harvest the leaves and flowers whenever they are available and the seeds from late summer. A pretty garden, border, container and conservatory herb.

USES Culinary, household, medicinal

Fenugreek is mainly grown as a salad herb and for its aromatic seeds. The leaves can also be cooked as a green vegetable. Dried fenugreek leaves contain coumarin and this sweet-smelling, hay-like scent makes the herb a good ingredient for pot-pourri mixtures. The slab-sided, light brown seeds, ground, resemble curry powder and so the powder is useful in Indian and oriental dishes. Tisanes can also be made from the seed and herbalists prescribe this as a tonic for stimulating digestion. Fenugreek seed also yields a yellow dye, suitable for dyeing cotton and wool.

Tropaeolum majus
Tropaeolaceae
NASTURTIUM

CULTIVATION A hardy annual with peppery-flavoured round leaves and trumpet-shaped, orange, yellow and red flowers. It grows to a height of 15–30cm (6–12in) and prefers poor, well-drained soil and full sun. Sow seeds in spring, 15–20cm (6–8in) apart. Good companion plants in kitchen gardens as their roots discourage soil pests and the flowers attract aphid-eating hover flies. Harvest the leaves and flowers when they are large enough to eat. Nasturtium is a delightful garden, border and container plant.
Recommended varieties
Dwarf, climbing and trailing types are ideal for most gardens, and the Atlantic hybrids have pretty, variegated leaves.

USES Culinary, cosmetic, household, medicinal

The nasturtium is a decorative plant native to Peru. Both the leaves and flowers have a high vitamin C content and the small leaves give a welcome piquancy to a green salad, while a handful of freshly-picked flowers strewn over the surface give a jewel-like brilliance to the dish. In the south of France, both the leaves and flowers are stuffed as you would vine leaves. Wine vinegar flavoured with nasturtium flowers develops a delicious peppery flavour and orange colour.

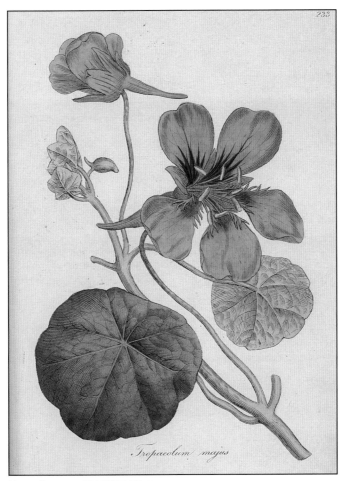

Tropaeolum majus, **NASTURTIUM**

Valeriana officinalis
Valerianaceae
VALERIAN

CULTIVATION This hardy herbaceous perennial has spear-shaped, bright green leaves and pink, white or rose-coloured flowers from midsummer. Growing to a height of 60cm–1.5m (2–5ft), it prefers poor, well-drained soil and full sun. It attracts earthworms, so use it in mixed borders and vegetable gardens. Propagate it by sowing seeds in spring or by dividing the plant in autumn, planting them 60cm (2ft) apart. Harvest the leaves and flowers from spring to autumn whenever they are available. A useful garden, border, container and conservatory herb.

USES Culinary, household, medicinal

Small young leaves of the herb can be added to a green salad and the flowers can be dried for use in herb wreaths. A tisane of valerian root acts as a sedative. When you are tidying the garden during the autumn, collect valerian leaves for adding to the compost heap.

Viola odorata
Violaceae
SWEET VIOLET

CULTIVATION This hardy deciduous perennial has small, green or purple, heart-shaped leaves and perfumed, velvety flowers of purple or white appearing during spring. It grows 10 to 15cm (4 to 6in) high and prefers fertile, moist soil and light shade. Propagate it from its runners or by dividing the plant during early autumn or late spring. Harvest the leaves and flowers whenever they are available. A pretty, traditional garden, border or edging herb.

USES Culinary, household, medicinal

The sweet violet's flowers appear during mild weather early in spring, usually half-hidden by the leaves. The French toss the sweet-tasting blooms over a salad of young leaves. Violet leaves taste good in a green salad and can be made into a tisane.

USEFUL ADDRESSES

HERB GARDENS

ABBEY DORE COURT,
Abbey Dore, Herefordshire

ABBEY HOUSE MUSEUM,
Leeds, West Yorkshire

ACORN BANK,
The National Trust, Cumbria

ALDERLEY GRANGE,
Alderley, Gloucestershire

ARLEY HALL AND GARDENS,
near Northwick, Cheshire

BARNSLEY HOUSE,
near Cirencester,
Gloucestershire

BATEMAN'S,
National Trust,
Burwash, East Sussex

BRAIDJULE,
Broughshane,
Ballymena, Northern Ireland

CAMBRIDGE BOTANIC GARDENS,
University Botanic Garden,
Cambridge

CAPEL MANOR,
Institute of Horticultural Field
Studies,
Waltham Cross, Hertfordshire

CASTLE DROGO,
near Chagford, Devon

CHELSEA PHYSIC GARDEN,
Chelsea, London

CHENIES MANOR HOUSE,
near Amersham,
Buckinghamshire

CLAVERTON MANOR AMERICAN

MUSEUM,
near Bath, Avon

CRANBORNE MANOR,
near Wimborne, Dorset

DARTINGTON HALL,
Totnes, Devon

DENMAN'S,
Fontwell, West Sussex

DOWER HOUSE (THE),
Badminton, Avon

ELLY HILL HERBS,
Elly Hill House, Barmpton,
Darlington, Durham

EMMANUEL COLLEGE,
Cambridge

EYHORNE MANOR,
Hollingborne, Kent

FELBRIGG HALL,
The National Trust,
Felbrigg, Norfolk

FULHAM PALACE,
Hammersmith, London SW6

GAULDEN MANOR,
Tolland,
near Taunton, Somerset

GLASGOW BOTANIC GARDENS,
Great Western Road, Glasgow,
Strathclyde, Scotland

GUNBY HALL,
The National Trust,
Burgh-le-Marsh,
near Spilsbury, Lincolnshire

HALL'S CROFT,
Old Town,
Stratford-upon-Avon,
Warwickshire

HARDWICK HALL,
Chesterfield, Derbyshire

HARLOW CAR GARDENS,
Harrogate, Yorkshire

HATFIELD HOUSE,
Hatfield, Hertfordshire

HESTERCOMBE HOUSE,
near Taunton, Somerset

HOLME PIERREPOINT HALL,
Nottinghamshire

HOPETOUN HOUSE,
South Queensferry,
Lothian, Scotland

IDEN CROFT NURSERIES AND
HERB FARM,
Staplehurst, Kent

IZAAK WALTON COTTAGE,
Shugborough, near Stafford

KNEBWORTH HOUSE,
Knebworth, Hertfordshire

KNOLE,
The National Trust,
Sevenoaks, Kent

LACKHAM COLLEGE OF
AGRICULTURE,
Lacock, Chippenham, Wiltshire

LINCOLN CATHEDRAL,
Lincoln

LITTLE MORETON HALL,
The National Trust,
Congleton, Cheshire

LYTES CARY MANOR,
Ilchester, Somerset

MALLORY COURT,
Leamington Spa, Warwickshire

MARLE PLACE,
Marle Place Plants, Brenchley,
near Tonbridge, Kent

MAWLEY HALL,
Cleobury Mortimer, Shropshire

MICHELHAMPTON PRIORY,
Upper Dicker, East Sussex

MOSELY OLD HALL,
Wolverhampton, West
Midlands

MOUNT STEWART GARDENS,
Newtonards,
County Down, Northern
Ireland

NESS GARDENS,
University of Liverpool Botanic
Gardens,
Ness Neston,
Wirral, Cheshire

NETHERBYRES,
Eyemouth, Borders, Scotland

NEW PLACE,
Chapel Street,
Stratford-upon-Avon,
Warwickshire

NOSEGAY GARDEN (THE),
Royal Botanic Gardens,
Kew, Surrey

OLD BARN (THE),
Fremington,
near Barnstaple, Devon

OLD RECTORY (THE),
Burghfield,
near Reading, Berkshire

OXBURGH HALL,
The National Trust,
Oxburgh,
near Swaffham, Norfolk

PETERBOROUGH CATHEDRAL,
Peterborough, Cambridgeshire

PRIORWOOD GARDEN,
The National Trust for
Scotland, Melrose, Borders,
Scotland

QUEEN'S GARDEN (THE),
Kew Palace,
Royal Botanic Gardens,
Kew, Surrey

ROYAL BOTANIC GARDEN,
Inverleith Road,
Edinburgh, Scotland

ROYAL HORTICULTURAL SOCIETY
GARDEN,
Wisley,
near Woking, Surrey

ST MICHAEL'S MOUNT,
Penzance, Cornwall

SHAKESPEARE GARDENS:
Anne Hathaway's Cottage,
Shottery, Stratford-upon-Avon,
Warwickshire

BIRTHPLACE GARDEN,
Henley Street, Stratford-upon-
Avon, Warwickshire

SCOTNEY CASTLE,
Lamberhurst, Kent

SISSINGHURST CASTLE,
Sissinghurst, Kent

SPRINGHILL,
The National Trust,
Moneymore,
County Londonderry,
Northern Ireland

STOCKFIELD PARK,
Wetherby, North Yorkshire

STONE COTTAGE,
Hambleton,
Oakham, Leicestershire

SUTTON MANOR,
Sutton Scotney,
near Winchester, Hampshire

THORNBY HERBS,
Thornby Hall Gardens,
Thornby, Northamptonshire

THREAVE GARDEN,
The National Trust for
Scotland, Castle Douglas,
Dumfries and Galloway,
Scotland

TRADESCANT GARDEN,
The Museum of Garden
History, Lambeth, London

TUDOR HOUSE (THE),
Southampton, Hampshire

WELSH FOLK MUSEUM,
National Museum of Wales,
St Fagans Castle
Cardiff, Wales

WEST GREEN HOUSE,
Hartley Witney, Hampshire

WESTMINSTER ABBEY HERB GARDEN,
Westminster Abbey,
London SW1

WHITTLESEA MUSEUM,
Market Street,
Whittlesey, Cambridgeshire

YORK GATE,
Back Church Lane,
Adel, Leeds

BIBLIOGRAPHY

Bardswell, Frances A., *The Herb Garden*, A.C. Black, 1911

Bremness, Lesley, *The Complete Book of Herbs*, Dorling Kindersley, 1988

Cooper, Guy; Taylor, Gordon; Bournsell, Clive, *English Herb Gardens*, Weidenfeld and Nicolson, 1986

Garland, Sarah, *The Herb Garden*, Windward, 1984

Grieve, Mrs M., *A Modern Herbal*, Penguin Handbooks, 1980

Hadfield, Miles, *A History of British Gardening*, Hutchinson and Company, 1960

Harvey, John, *Medieval Gardens*, B.T. Batsford Ltd, 1981

Holt, Geraldene, *The Gourmet Garden*, Pavilion/Little, Brown and Company, 1990
Recipes from a French Herb Garden, Conran Octopus/Simon & Schuster, 1989

Hopkinson, Simon and Judith, *Herbs, their care and cultivation*, Cassell, 1990

Larkcom, Joy, *The Salad Garden*, Frances Lincoln/Windward, 1984

Le Rougetel, Hazel, *The Chelsea Gardener, Philip Miller 1691–1771*, Natural History Museum, 1990

Lowenfeld, Claire, *Herb Gardening*, Faber and Faber, 1964

McLean, Teresa, *Medieval English Gardens*, William Collins, 1981

Masefield, G.B., Wallis, M., Harrison, S.G., Nicholson, B.E., *The Oxford Book of Food Plants*, Oxford University Press, 1969

Paterson, Allen, *Herbs in the Garden*, J.M. Dent and Sons Ltd., 1985

Peplow, Elizabeth and Reginald, *Herbs and Herb Gardens*, Webb and Bower, 1984

Phillips, Roger and Foy, Nicky, *Herbs*, Pan Original, 1990

INDEX

ACKNOWLEDGMENTS

AUTHOR'S ACKNOWLEDGMENTS

Years before I had agreed to write a book about herbs I was well aware of the daunting size of the subject and its considerable literature. No group of plants can have been better documented, or for longer. This book, though, makes no claims to be encyclopaedic; it is simply a personal view of the herbs I grow and the pleasure they give me.

While working on the book I have received much kindness and generosity from many gardeners, cooks and herbalists. The staff of both the Lindley Library and Wisley Gardens of the Royal Horticultural Society have been patient and helpful. I should particularly like to acknowledge the valuable assistance of several friends. They have photographed gardens, obtained books and recipes and even sent parcels of fresh herbs from as far as Australia, Cyprus, North America, France and Scotland. I thank them all most warmly: Myrtle and Dorinna Allen, Elizabeth Baker, Rosemary Barron, Anna Best, Claire Clifton, Colin Capon, Jeannette and Suzanne Doize, Lisa Kalaydjian, Efterpi Kyriacou, Patsy Guyer, Nevin Halici, Richard Hoskins, Laura Hudson, Allen Lacy, Janette Marshall, Sri Owen, Maro Pambou, Christalla Pantelides, Claudia Roden, Cherry Ripe, Lazaros Sparsis and Julie Toll. Finally my affection and gratitude goes to my husband and children who tirelessly collected information, seeds and plants.

PUBLISHER'S ACKNOWLEDGMENTS

The publisher would like to thank the following people for their help in preparing this book:

Michael and Denny Wickham, Clock House, Coleshill, Nr. Swindon, Wiltshire; Simon Hopkinson of Hollington Nurseries; Mr and Mrs A.J. Radcliffe; Essebourne Manor, Berkshire; Ragna Tischler Goddard; Hollington Herbs, Woolton Hill, Newbury, Berkshire; Mr and Mrs M. Hale; Jane Croswell-Jones of The Grange, Whatley Vineyard, Whatley, Frome, Somerset; Lynne Robinson; Richard Lowther; Lin and David Lobb, Hayford Hall.

Special thanks to the following people for providing props for special photography:

The Hop Shop, Castle Farm, Shoreham, Sevenoaks, Kent; Stitches & Daughters, 5–7 Tranquil Vale, Blackheath Village, London SE3; Gallery of Antique Costume & Textiles, 2 Church Street, London NW8; Tobias & The Angel, 68 White Hart Lane, Barnes, London SW13; The Shaker Shop, 25 Harcourt Street, London W1; Enigma (stand 22), Persiflage (stand 25), Chenil Galleries, 181–183 Kings Road, London SW3; Perfect Glass, 5 Park Walk, London SW10; Ashill Colour Studio, Clovers, Church Street, Alcombe, Minehead, Somerset.

And special thanks also to all those people in England and France who very kindly permitted photography to take place in their homes and gardens.

PICTURE ACKNOWLEDGMENTS

1 Jerry Harpur (Essebourne Manor, Berkshire); 2 Marie Claire Beautes/Le Mene; 8 Georges Lévêque; 10–11 Clay Perry; 14 Angelo Hornak; 15 Royal Botanic Gardens, Kew; 16–17 Private Collection/Bridgeman Art Library; 18 Jacqui Hurst/Boys Syndication; 19 Heather Angel (designer: Tim Martin); 20–1 Jerry Harpur (designer: Jane Fearnley-Whittingstall); 21 right Jacqui Hurst/Boys Syndication; 23 Georges Lévêque; 24–5 Stephen Robson/National Trust Picture Library; 25 right Georges Lévêque (Etta de Haes, The Netherlands); 26 Michèle Lamontagne; 27 Jerry Pavia/Garden Picture Library; 28 Tania Midgley; 29 Clive Boursnell/Garden Picture Library; 30–1 Jerry Pavia/Garden Picture Library; 33 Georges Lévêque (Chilcombe House); 34 above S. & O. Mathews; 34 below Brigitte Thomas (Denmans); 35 Karen Bussolini; 38 Karen Bussolini; 40–1 Gary Rogers; 41 right Andrew Lawson; 41 below Jacqui Hurst/Boys Syndication; 42 Michèle Lamontagne; 43 Georges Lévêque (Samares Manor, Jersey); 44–6 Jerry Harpur (Mr & Mrs A.J. Radcliffe); 48–50 Brigitte Thomas (Haseley Court); 52–4 Karen Bussolini (designer: Ragna Tischler Goddard); 56–8 Jerry Harpur (Essebourne Manor, Berkshire); 64 La Maison de Marie Claire/Godeaut/Lebeau; 65 Di Lewis/Elizabeth Whiting and Associates; 66 Paul Ryan/J.B. Visual Press; 72–91 Angelo Hornak (Courtesy of the collections of The Lindley Library, Vincent Square and the Royal Botanic Gardens, Kew).

The following photographs were specially taken for Conran Octopus by Debbie Patterson: 5, 6–7, 12–13, 22, 32, 36–7, 60–1, 62, 63, 70–71.